Integrating Agile Scrum into the Waterfall Process

By Anita Rosen

Anita Rosen

Integrating Agile Scrum into the Waterfall Process

ISBN: 9781520369518

Cover design by Robin Ludwig Design Inc., www.gobookcoverdesign.com
Text copyright © Anita Rosen 2017, All rights reserved

Table of Contents

Preface 1

Introduction 1

   Benefits of a Defined and Combined Process: 2

   Waterfall and Scrum Basics 3

   Comparing Different Frameworks 4

   Phases in the Waterfall/Scrum Process 4

   Waterfall/Scrum Team Members 5

Phase 1 - Initiation 8

   Phase 1 Overview 8

   Reviewing Product Ideas 9

   The Business Plan 11

      Product Feasibility 11

      Product Goals 14

      Client's Needs 17

      Product Environment 23

      Product Backlog 25

      Estimating Product Costs 26

      Estimated Potential Revenue 29

   Phase 1 – Initiation – Presentation 30

      About the Phase 1 Presentation 30

      The Phase 1 Presentation Includes: 31

   Recommendations for Management and Team Members 31

      Recommendations for Management 31

   Documents Created in Phase 1 33

      By Document 33

      By Department 33

Phase 2 – Planning 35

   Phase 2 Objective 35

- The Players in Phase 2 35
- The Planning Phase 36
- Creating a Team 37
- Getting Started: 38
- Creating Team Minutes 41
- Development's Role in Phase 2 42
- The Design Review 44
- Team Member's – What Everyone Else Is Doing 46
  - Roll Out Plan 47
- Updating the Product Backlog 48
- Product Flow from Development through Release: 48
  - Development Flow 49
  - The Definition of Done 50
  - Moving an increment to Beta: 50
- Creating the Integrated Schedule 50
  - A Better Way: 51
- Running the Session: 51
- Managing Change: 53
- Creating a Base Line Cost Document 54
- Outsourcing 57
- Phase 2– Planning – Presentation 58
  - Sample Phase 2 Presentation Outline: 59
- Recommendations for Management and Team Members 59
- Summary of Deliverables for Phase – 2 – Planning 60
- Phase 2 Summary by department 61
- Documents Created in Phase 2 62

Phase 3 – Scrum-Development 65

- Project Team Members: 65
- Scrum Team Members: 66
- Scrum Framework: 67
  - How The Scrum Process Works: 67

    Product Backlog Refinement 69
Project Team Tasks 71
    Moving Increments to Beta 71
    The Beta Plan 72
    Identifying Beta Clients 74
Evaluating Vendors 75
The Release Plan 76
The Announcement Plan 77
The Phase 3 – Development – Presentation 80
    Sample Phase 3 Presentation Outline: 81
    Recommendations for Management and Team Members 82
    Summary of Deliverables by Department in Phase 3 82
    Documents Created in Phase 3 Development 84

Phase 4 – Beta 85
Phase 4 – Beta Players 86
Monitored Release Product 87
Ending Beta 88
Recommendations for Management and the Team 88
    Team Member's Roles 89

Phase 5 – General Availability 90
The Player's in Phase 5 are: 90
Product Release 91
During General Availability: 92
Phase 5 – General Availability – Review Presentation 94
Sample Phase 5 Presentation Outline: 94
Recommendations for Management and Team Members 95
Team Member's Roles 95
Documents Created In Phase 5 96

Phase 6 – End of Life 97
What Happens During End of Life 97
Phase 6 – EOL Presentation 98

Sample Phase 6 presentation outline: 98
Recommendations for Management and Team Members 99
Team Member's Roles 99
Documents Created In Phase 6 100
Index 101
Scrum Definitions: 101
Phases in the Process 102
Product Team Members 103
Documents Created by Phase 104
    Phase 1: Initiation 104
    Phase 2: Planning 104
    Phase 3: Scrum Development 105
Sources Sited in this Book: 106

Preface

The hybridization of scrum with other software development methodologies is common as scrum does not cover the whole product development lifecycle; therefore, organizations find the need to add in additional processes to create a more comprehensive implementation. – Wikipedia

Is your organization moving to Scrum? Are you new to project management and your developers use Scrum? Have you moved to Scrum but you find something lacking? – Then this book is for you.

Integrating Agile Scrum into the Waterfall Process provides a step-by-step implementation. This book can be used to learn what is expected in each product development phase, what documents are to be created, team member's responsibilities, along with practical, real world, suggestions, and hints to better manage people and process. Now your continually released products can come out on time, on budget, and with the features customers want.

Changes need to be made to an existing Waterfall process when organizations incorporate Scrum and move their project development from a sequential environment to an iterative one. By realigning Waterfall to flow into and support the Scrum framework, continuously released products can be effectively and efficiently managed.

Waterfall and Scrum frameworks are complementary. Waterfall provides an excellent model for managing a product through its life cycle. Waterfall does not identify best practices for managing the development process; – Scrum does.

Integrating Agile Scrum into the Waterfall Process has been designed for a Project Manager, a Product Owner, a ScrumMaster, or anyone else involved with Product Lifecycle Management.

If you have questions or need support in implementing your product life cycle needs, please contact me via my website: anitarosen.com

Anita Rosen

Introduction

To begin with, **Waterfall** is a *sequential process*, where an idea is identified, a design is developed, the product is created, and then the product is released.

More recently organizations are incorporating the Agile Scrum framework to develop products. **Agile Scrum** is an *iterative process*, whereby small teams continually develop working increments of a product.

The adaption of Scrum has come about due to changing business needs. In traditional development, organizations set a release date, then run through a sequential process. For projects that don't have a beginning, middle, and end, an iterative process can be more effective.

A typical, traditional, waterfall project would be a physical project. For example, when Apple plans a new iPhone, they set a date for the announcement, decide on a set of features, then create a cross-functional team to makes this happen.

This life cycle is different than what is needed for a product that is continually released. Many web driven products, like Facebook's site, are continually updated. Web-based applications have no planned date for a release announcement since iterations of these applications are continually being created, modified, updated, and released. In this continual release cycle, a cross-functional team responsible for a set of functions or features will choose which tasks they can complete in a month or less time-block. At the end of each time-block, their work is inspected to assure it meets a pre-set definition, and then the product is moved to the release process. This process is continually repeated.

On the surface, one would think that Waterfall and Scrum are mutually exclusive processes. But in reality, they are complimentary. That is, Waterfall has very little to say on how to manage development, while Scrum provides no framework for identifying and prioritizing projects, designing projects, releasing, or providing end of life for a project. Combining both of these processes together can create a more detailed and effective framework. As stated by Scrum.org in The Scrum Guide:

> *Scrum is only about projects and there should be another system for managing programs and portfolios. – The Scrum Guide*

The goal of this book is to provide a guide for organizations to combine Waterfall and Scrum.

Benefits of a Defined and Combined Process:

This book's goal is to provide a roadmap for integrating Scrum into a Waterfall process. Included are best use practices that detail why procedures and deliverables are created. This allows an organization to create an informed, intelligent, decision-making process. Below are a series of common questions followed by answers.

Why use Scrum for development; why not continue with your current process?
- Will features and functionality of a project change between Initiation and release? If so, a framework that supports this dynamic environment is needed.
- A better development workflow management system is needed.
- It is preferable to release increments of a product instead of waiting for the entire product to be completed.

How to know if a combined Waterfall/Scrum process is needed?
- A complete product lifecycle process is needed, not just a development process.
- Currently Waterfall and Scrum teams are fighting for control. There has to be a better way to manage this process.
- Management is looking to implement Scrum alongside an existing Waterfall process. A guide line for implementation is needed.
- It always seems that every product release is a scramble. No one ever really knows what is going to be in the final product or when the product will actually be released until the date it is released. How can projects be better planned?
- Product decisions seem to be made in the hallways. There never is a forum where all the facts can be laid out and discussed. How can the process be better managed?
- A continually released product is running into roadblocks due to lack of design and architecture. How to better plan for future products.

Why have a set Waterfall/Scrum process?
- A process ensures that everyone knows what is expected of them, when it is expected, where they get information from, and to whom they give information.
- Better execution of products.
- Shortening of the development process and providing client departments with more insight into the steps necessary to create an effective new solution.

- With a defined process there is less chance for surprises, fires, and core features are not forgotten.
- A defined process ensures prerequisites to be completed when needed since employees understand what is expected of them. Processes are already created so they don't need to be recreated for each product.
- For the executive, having a clear process provides the tools to focus on strategic direction instead of worrying about implementation.
- Many products are the result of a great idea. Execution can provide the difference between a successful product and one that does not meet client's needs, comes in late, or over budget.
- Many organizations think they don't need processes because they are too small or that a documented process is too bureaucratic. Any size organization needs to plan its products properly. Executives need to be focused on driving business direction not making sure individual contributors know what to do next.
- A written corporate process provides an organization with a definition of what is created, why it is created, when it is created.

Waterfall and Scrum Basics

Before getting started, let's define Waterfall, Scrum, and a few terms used throughout this book.

Scrum - Scrum is an iterative and incremental Agile software development framework for managing product development.

Waterfall - The waterfall model is a sequential process, in which progress is seen as flowing steadily downwards (like a waterfall) through the phases.

Waterfall/Scrum – is the process of identifying, designing, developing, releasing, and managing a product. The Waterfall/Scrum model is made up of a series of distinct phases. Employees throughout the organization may become involved with the project at various times throughout the product's lifecycle.

Product – This book uses Product to refer to the actual component being created.

Project – This book uses Project to refer to the process of creating a product.

Comparing Different Frameworks

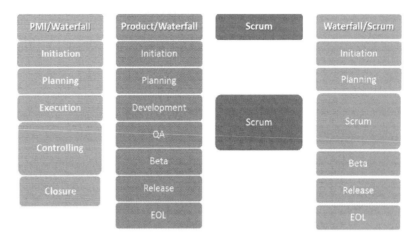

Figure 0-1 – Comparing Waterfall, Scrum, and the combined process.

Phases in the Waterfall/Scrum Process

The adage goes, how do you eat an elephant … one bite at a time. The same applies to developing a product. The best way to create a product is to break it into manageable units. This book consists of six sections. Each section represents one phase of the product lifecycle.

Phase 1 – Initiation – All ideas must be vetted. Initiation is the stage when the Business Plan is created and presented. The objective of Phase 1 is to introduce a new product idea or next generation idea to the organization, to gain agreement on relevance to strategic direction, to produce a Business Plan whereby executive staff receives a snapshot of the products costs, market reach, features, scope, and potential revenue. This way management can decide if it's beneficial for the organization to fund this product.

Phase 2 – Planning – The objective of Phase 2 is to define, architect, prototype, and design a product that satisfies the business plan identified in Phase 1. In Phase 2 the product architecture, a Development Cost Baseline, and a Project Team is formed.

Phase 3 – Scrum-Development – Following the Scrum framework, the Development Team creates increments of the product by choosing items off of the prioritized Product Backlog. Each increment will work within the structure of the design created in Phase 2. The Development Team is responsible for creating, testing and quality assuring that each increment works to the definition of Done that has been mutually agreed on by all parties. After each increment has met the definition of Done, the Project Team will identify if the increment is ready to be released to Beta.

Phase 4 – Beta –After the Project Team decides that an increment, story, or epic is ready to be released, it is made available to a select group of Clients who have agreed to confirm that the features work in a production environment.

Phase 5 – General Availability – After the Beta, when the team has confirmed that the increment works in a production environment, the increment becomes generally available.

Phase 6 – End of Life – At the yearly product review meeting, management may decide that the product has become obsolete or more expensive to support than the benefit generated from use. End of Life is the process whereby the product's history can be reviewed and a decision can be made regarding whether or not a product should be discontinued.

Waterfall/Scrum Team Members

Waterfall/Scrum projects will have two teams, the Project Team, and the Scrum Team. The number of people on a Project Team will depend on the size and visibility of the product. Whatever the size of the Project Team, the same functions need to be executed. The difference between small products and large products is the scope. That is if you are a programmer in your bedroom you will be performing all of the roles outlined below. If you are in a large organization, a member of each department will be representing their area of responsibility.

Clients – are not actually on a team but so important to the success of a product they need to be thought of as a silent team member. They are the people who will use what the team is developing. Clients may be employees, partners, customers, or the general public.

Client Support – is responsible for defining, designing, and developing a detailed plan that articulates how the organization will support a product or increment after it is released. The Support Plan defines how Client Support staff will be trained, clients will access help, how bugs will be tracked and fixed after release, the training available to clients, and how updates/fixes will be sent to clients.

Development Manager – the functional area responsible for managing Development. They serve on the Project Team and provide costing, project plans, and interdepartmental direction. They do not manage the Development Team.

Development Team – is a self-managing, cross-functional team made up of 3- 9 people. A product can have multiple Development Teams. Each team works from a common Product Backlog. Each Development Team defines, designs, develops, performs testing, quality assures, documents and fixes any errors for each increment of the product they create.

Documentation – the functional area responsible for documenting increments. The actual writer is a member of the Development Team, while a Documentation Manager serves on the Project Team and provides costing, project plans, and interdepartmental direction.

Marketing Communications – is the functional area responsible for all communications inside and outside of the organization. Smaller organizations do not need a separate communications person for internal products; the Project Manager will handle all the internal corporate communication. Larger organizations, with offices scattered around the country, or around the globe, most likely will have a person whose responsibility is to provide communications to internal clients. If the increment will be made available to clients outside of the organization, corporate communications will interact with public relations (PR), advertising, industry analysts, bloggers, and other outside agencies.

Product Owner - The person responsible for representing the client and other stakeholders and managing the Product Backlog. For projects that are delivered to an external Client the Product Owner typically is the Product Manager. For internal Projects the Product Owner is typically from the Client organization.

Product Marketing – is responsible for product direction, industry analysis, competitive analysis, understanding the client's needs and identifying and driving product direction. Product Marketing works with all areas within the organization to make sure the product is focused on the client and is presented in the best possible light.

Project Manager – is responsible for making sure each member of the Project Team understands his/her interdependencies. The Project Manager facilitates communications among departments. They manage processes and confirm that the deliverables within each stage of the product lifecycle have been met. When deliverables slip, it is the responsibility of the Project Manager to escalate this information and to facilitate resolution. In smaller organizations, the Product Manager's duties usually incorporate those of Product Marketing and Marketing Communications.

Quality Assurance – is the area responsible for running tests to assure each increment meets the organization's quality standard. The person who performs quality assurance is on the Development Team, while a Quality Assurance Manager serves on the Project Team. Where they provide costing, project plans, and interdepartmental direction.

ScrumMaster - The person responsible for facilitating the Scrum process. The Scrum Master is responsible for representing the Scrum Team and Scrum Process at all Project Team meetings. For projects that have multiple Development Teams, each Scrum Master or one Scrum Master representing all the Development Teams attends the Project Team Meeting.

Scrum Team - Each Scrum Team is made up of a Development Team, a Scrum Master and a Product Owner.

Training – is responsible for providing classroom and online training materials, based on Client Support and Product Marketing requirements. They will provide costing, project plans and attend Project Team meetings.

Phase 1 - Initiation

All new products or major new versions of an existing product should be evaluated to make sure they strategically fit the organization's direction. Phase 1 provides the forum for introducing new product ideas and for new versions of an existing product to obtain approval to build a Business Plan.

Phase 1 is broken into two steps.
- Step 1: an idea is presented to management for approval
- Step 2: once approved, the idea is vetted for feasibility

After approval, a Phase 1 Lead and a Development Lead will be appointed. The Phase 1 Lead writes the Business Plan. The Development Lead provides technical input.

Phase 1 Overview

The objective of Phase 1 is to introduce a new product idea or next generation version to the organization, to gain agreement on relevance to strategic direction, to produce a Business Plan, and for executive staff to receive a snapshot of the product's cost and revenue so that management can decide if it is beneficial for the organization to develop this product.

Many products are standard operating procedures. These tend to be software updates and roll-outs of new hardware. Many organizations have a timetable they live buy. This timetable outlines what software will be updated and how often the hardware needs to be updated. For existing applications, this is a very effective strategy to ensure that current applications and equipment are managed efficiently. This is different than a new idea or a new initiative.

A new product idea can come from anywhere. There are many ways a new idea comes to light. The first part of this chapter outlines one foolproof process that can be used to identify the viability of a Initiation.

One of the black holes in many organizations is the process whereby new products come into being. Many times a senior executive identifies a new trend and spearheads an initiative to execute. Other product ideas are a reaction to competitors or industry issues. Some products bubble up from Client Support or employee complaints. Many times products find their way into IT after renegade departments purchase hardware and software then need IT to manage their solution.

We hear about kids making millions off of an app they created in their bedroom or dorm room. Out of the hundreds of thousands of apps that are being created this way, very few gain traction and even fewer turn into a viable company. The people who "just create" and become successful will tell others that there is no need for a process. For an app to have more than a million-to-one shot at working properly and meeting client's needs, a formal vetting process is a good start.

To do this, a forum needs to be created where all potential ideas are presented. The people who attend this forum need to have the authority to fund the second part of Initiation. At the end of this forum, a number of ideas will have been approved to go forward. Each of these ideas will need to be vetted. That is a Phase 1 Lead will be assigned to create a Business Plan. Creating a Business Plan is as important for products that bubble up as it is for ideas that are being led by a senior executive.

The Phase 1 Lead can come from many different disciplines within the organization. They may come from a Business Development group, Product Marketing, Project Management, or Development. They may have multiple responsibilities or in Phase 2, turn into the Product Manager. If the Phase 1 Lead does not come from Development, a Development Lead will need to be identified. The Phase 1 Lead will provide the Development Lead with their assessment of client needs and proposed features. The Development Lead will review the idea and provide a ballpark of how difficult it will be to achieve the idea and how long it will take to execute the idea.

Reviewing Product Ideas

On a defined schedule, a team with authority should hold meetings to review all submitted ideas and see which ideas look promising. The frequency of these meetings are based on the size of your organization, need for change, and the number of ideas requested. Keep the idea proposals simple. The focus of these meetings is not to fund the product, it is to review proposed ideas and identify which ideas should have a Business Plan created.

Many organizations leave this step out since they think it adds too much bureaucracy. Don't succumb to this thinking. A process makes it easier for an organization to look for trends and identify new ideas. It is worthwhile looking at all ideas that are submitted. There might be a theme to submitted ideas that could highlight trends before they become issues.

Once the ideas have been reviewed, the top ideas are given to a Phase 1 Lead who is tasked with creating a Business Plan.

> *It's True: After an idea has been submitted, the first step in actualizing a Business Plan is to have a clear understanding of the request.*

Reviewing ideas that are from within the organization can provide insights into inefficiencies and help the organization create best use practices. Many times employees who are using existing applications on a day-to-day basis have good insight and recommendations on how to better streamline the processes they use. Employees may request that screens be simplified, information saved can be easier accessed, that information can be easily sorted by specific fields. Clients may be calling Sales asking for information that exists in the corporate database but is not displayed on Sales' tablet or smartphone, or the information could be directly served to Clients, streamlining the sales job.

Many times departments within an organization get frustrated with an existing process and go around the system, purchasing new equipment and software so that they can better perform their job. Currently, many employees use their personal Smartphones or tablets for work. IT is now playing catch up, making sure existing applications work properly and safely on these devices. This phenomenon isn't new. Back in the 1980's PC's entered most organizations through the back door. When employees had problems and needed help they turned to IT. Reluctantly IT took ownership of corporate PCs. When the Internet crept into organizations in the 1990's, most IT organizations had learned their lesson and were fast to take control so that they could provide employees with Internet access, corporate security, and the creation of intranet sites.

Many times new employees, those who have worked with other organizations, have had different experiences using tools that make their job easier or provide better services to clients. Organizations can leverage these experiences to create more efficient applications.

> *It's True: Ideas that come from employee experiences need to be written down and submitted to the organization. The organization needs a methodology to capture and vet these ideas.*

Keep this process simple. To start with, an idea proposal process will need to be created. An easy way to implement the gathering of ideas is to create a simple fill in form on your organization's intranet whereby employees can provide requests and propose solutions. This might include a space for proposed idea, organization saving, organization and employee benefit. Periodically requests created by this form should be reviewed for viability. Frequent requests, those that provide a high rate of return or cost savings can be vetted to see if they are feasible and should be funded. Once a product idea has been approved by the vetting process, a Phase 1 Lead is identified and is tasked with creating a Business Plan.

The Business Plan

Every new idea and major update needs a Business Plan. This plan is made up of the following elements.
- Feasibility
- Goal
- Client's Needs
- Product Environment
- Product Backlog
- Estimated Product Costs
- Potential Revenue

Product Feasibility

Many ideas' sound good on paper but are not a good fit for the organization. Initially, ideas need to be reviewed to assure feasibility. The following is an example of a simple list that products should be reviewed against.
- Is the infrastructure created by this product reusable?
- Is the product based on technology the organization is already using and currently has expertise in-house?
- Can the product be developed using off the shelf applications, known technology, or will your Development organization need to be inventing new technologies?
- Will the new product slip seamlessly into your current employee or external client offerings or will you need to install additional hardware and provide additional training or identify a new customer market?
- If the organization is set up as a profit center is the product's ROI (return on investment) or margin acceptable?

Figuring out a Product's Feasibility

Many ideas sound good on paper but are not a good fit for the organization. For instance, the organization may lack the sophistication to implement and run a technically complicated application, or an application may require a very structured approach that does not match with the organization's operations.

First identify all the departments in a released product's sphere, then identify if this new product uses new or existing infrastructure and resources. The chart below is an example of a product that uses existing Development infrastructure but will need new Sales, Support, and Marketing infrastructure.

Department	New	Existing
Sales	Yes	No
Equipment	No	Yes
Development	No	Yes
Customer Support	Yes	No
Marketing	Yes	No

Figure 1-1 Resource Table

Then plot where your product falls using the chart below. The horizontal bar identifies Development's knowledge. The vertical bar identifies Client access. The Client bar can also be used for Sales' reach. That is if the sales team has experience selling a product or has external client contacts who purchase this type of product.

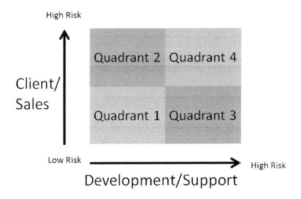

Figure 1- 2 Resource Matrix

The lowest risk products are in quadrant 1; this is where both Development and Clients are familiar and knowledgeable about developing or using a product. While the highest risk products are in quadrant 4, this is where Development and Clients are unfamiliar and will need additional training.

Quadrant 1 – The proposed solution will use technologies already familiar to your Development organization. The proposed solution will be familiar to your Client community or Sales will be selling to existing clients.

Quadrant 2 – A product that takes advantage of existing skills found within your existing Development organization and uses familiar equipment, but this solution will change the way your Client community works. For example, Clients will need extensive training or new equipment, or your sales team will need to find new external clients.

Quadrant 3 – A product where Development will need to purchase new technology, train or hire new programmers, architect or design a solution that has never been done before (high-risk technology); while the solution will be sold to existing clients with minimal if any training.

Quadrant 4 – A high-risk solution that requires extensive training for Development, Sales, and Clients.

The highest success rates and lowest hidden costs will be for those products found in quadrant 1. As products move out of quadrant 1 and into quadrants 2, 3, and 4, risks increase as the unknowns, learning curves, and purchases increase. It is important to understand up front a product's level of risk since, higher risk products typically have higher hidden costs, may take longer to implement, and are at a higher risk to miss targeted savings or revenue.

Quadrant 1 example: Development Team adds a new feature to an existing application. Both Development and the Client community are familiar with the hardware and software used.

Quadrant 2 example: The organization is adding a new application that will be deployed on Smartphones and tablets. Clients already have these devices and know how to use them. Development does not have experience in developing a Smartphone graphic user interface (GUI), programming languages, databases, or the equipment being deployed.

Quadrant 3 example: If the vertical axes represents Sales – Sales currently sells into HR departments. The new product uses similar technology but is sold directly to consumers. Sales will need to create a whole new selling model.

Quadrant 4 example: Your current Development organization is familiar with Microsoft OS and uses Microsoft Visual Studio while this new project needs Developers who are familiar with Apple's Xcode. While your sales organization sells to corporate clients and this new product is sold to consumers.

Look at the infrastructure created by this product. If Development consists of C# or Java programmers and this product needs Swift or Objective-C programmers, how difficult or how much time will it take to hire new programmers or train your existing programmers for this new environment? Likewise, if the Client Support organization currently needs to be proficient in database management and this new product needs people proficient in data communications, this product may cost more than anticipated. When departmental managers put together their plans, they'll need to include training and cross-functional support. Specifically, Client Support employees may not have the skills to cover for one another, adding costs to the product roll out.

Cost effective products typically reuse internal infrastructure, allowing existing and new employees to easily migrate between products. When migrating your existing applications to take advantage of new technology, this product may require that you migrate existing employee skill sets. Identify, up front, if you need to change the skill set of existing employees,. You will need to factor in the cost and time of training.

Early into this process, you will need to identify skill sets necessary for the product to be successful. If your plan is to make an existing app work on a mobile platform, then developers who have worked on previous, non-mobile, versions of the application may bring more to the table then hiring a recent college graduate who is proficient with Java or Swift. Development will need to figure into its cost the time it will take to get existing employees educated on new technologies. This education process should be started once Initiation is approved. The Planning phase will give Development the time to send employees to training classes and, if necessary, hire additional people who can augment the team with their experience.

Finally, the organization should look at the project's ability to reuse known technology. When creating a new technology, it is wise to limit the number of unknowns. Creating new technology based on new technology can lead to a disaster. Many organizations have learned this the hard way. There are many stories of programmers designing solutions based on a vendor's non-disclosure presentation. The organization reaches a critical point in the development process only to realize the infrastructure technology they need does not exist. The Resource matrix is one tool that management can use to assess the risk of a product.

Product Goals

The basis for any successful product is creating effective product goals.
- Goals drive a product
- Goals are used to focus a product
- Goals give the team the perspective they need to effectively create a product
- Goals bring disparate groups together
- Goals provide a metric for success

Goals – Step 1—Identify Your Stakeholders

Every product has multiple stakeholders. The first step in creating goals is to identify who are the product's stakeholders and each of their goals. Each stakeholder has a different goal. The three most common stakeholders are executive management, the department requesting the product, and the client. For a product to be successful each stakeholder's needs must be identified and met.

Examples of goals for each stakeholder:

Executive Management – Internal product: efficiency, keeping down costs and increasing employee productivity. External product: revenue generation, client loyalty, market leadership, or cost savings.

Sales: Saves time, provides better lead generation. External product: drives clients to use your products and services, provides better services.

Client – Saves time or provides timely information they can't get elsewhere.

It is the responsibility of the Phase 1 Lead to figure out who each of the stakeholders is and to provide benefits for each stakeholder. This is a small but worthwhile exercise. Each idea gets three stakeholders: management, the department that benefits or is responsible for the product, and the client, along with a few words that describe their benefit. If the Phase 1 Lead cannot easily identify the stakeholders or their benefits, this is a sign that the idea should not proceed.

Goals – Step 2 – Make The Goals Measurable And Actionable.

Too many times goals are created that are not measurable or actionable. Examples of goals that are NOT measurable and actionable are: Create an app, reduce costs, improve sales, make money … For goals to be effective they need to be measurable and actionable. That is, a date and an action of what will be achieved by that date needs to be present. This allows the Project Team to go back to their goals to see if the organization is meeting targets.

Example 1:
Not a Goal: Increase field access to corporate scheduling
Goal: **100% of employees** with a Smartphone have access to corporate scheduling **by 3Q**
3rd quarter – actionable
100% of employees – measurable
Example 2:
Not a Goal: Give employee's iPhones
Goal: **90%** of sales force has an iPhone **by September**
September – actionable

90% of salesforce - measurable

Example 3:

Not a Goal: Provide an account management app to our clients

Goal: **5,000 clients** have downloaded our account management app **by April**

April – is actionable

5,000 clients have downloaded – is measurable

Example 4:

Not a Goal: Collect client data

Goal: Collect client data so that **one year after the mobile app goes live** client use patterns for the **next 24 hours** have been identified.

One year after the app goes live – measurable;

Client's behavior for the next 24 hour after an action – actionable

This goal provides a focus for the data scientists.

All measurable and actionable goals include numbers. Effective goals clearly specify what is going to happen and when it's going to happen. Without numbers there is no goal – it's just a nebulous statement. Many people in an organization are scared of measurable and actionable goals. They are afraid of being measured, they are afraid of not meeting the goal. Don't let these people do away with numbers. If necessary, make the goals less scary by making them more achievable. If a manager doesn't like 100%, find what number they feel comfortable with.

Step 3 – Prioritizing and Ranking Your Goals

A product should have three to five goals. The next step after creating product goals is to prioritize and rank them. For each goal, identify if it will be easy, medium, or hard to obtain. Then rank the goals from most important to least important. Why is a goal hard to achieve? Is it access to technology? Hiring people with the right skills? Getting people trained? Internal politics? Budgets? Getting the word out? If the goal is broken in two, can part of it be easy while the other part is hard?

> *It's True: If this project includes data mining, A common mistake management makes is to expect the data scientists to set the goals for data mining. The data scientist(s) will mine for whatever patterns they can find, instead of focusing their searches on patterns that are meaningful to the organization. Clearly stating what is hoped from data mining can positively influence the effectiveness of the project.*

Hints for Making Goals Easier To Achieve:

- By lowering the number from 100% to 80% will the goal more achievable? By moving the date from January to May, will it be more achievable? Do you need to keep low ranked goals that are hard to achieve?
- Whenever you identify a hard goal, create a separate page called "Possible Road Blocks". This will give management and the team insight into possible future issues.
- Goals are used to keep the team focused on what they are achieving.

Tip: Review goals at each stage of the Product Life Cycle to assure the team is maintaining focus and that the goals are still valid and accurate.

Client's Needs

This section of the Business Plan identifies the client's needs and effects the product will have on the organization.
- This section is the fundamental building block of a good product.
- Without a thorough business assessment at Initiation time the best designed and executed product will not necessarily produce any results.
- Clearly identified Client's Needs provides insight into the end clients and their requirements.

Tip: don't shortcut the process. Documenting clients' needs provides the organization with the necessary information to create an effective product. Don't turn a molehill into a mountain. This section of the Business Plan can be as simple as a one sentence answer for each of the following questions.

Every product, regardless the size or level of complication needs to define the Client. The Phase 1 Lead creates a document identifying the following information:
- Who are the clients?
- Why do they need this new product?
- How will this affect them?
- How will this affect the way they currently work?
- What additional training if any, will they need?

- What features do they need in the eventual solution (list the top five features)?
- What benefit(s) will they obtain from this product?

There are many products created without defining Client's Needs. When asked why this section of the Business Plan doesn't exist the typical response is, this information was intuitively obvious or it seemed so bureaucratic to write it down. It is very important to identify the client regardless of the size of the product or the size of the organization. From a product that is derived from a hackathon to a full blown corporate initiative, the preceding questions need to be answered. This information solidifies the products position. Having the information written down explains and verifies the decision-making process.

Many times the people involved during Initiation are no longer involved with the product or are with the organization later in the product cycle. Ideas that seemed intuitive today may not look intuitive in the future. Additionally, many times people believe they are in agreement. Later, they all believe that their recollection is correct, even though none of the recollections are the same.

Information written down confirms that ideas discussed are in agreement. The information identified in the Client's Needs section is the basis for all decisions made throughout the product's lifecycle. Many products evolve over time. A written document provides a clear record identifying when the product changes and provides new players with the product's history.

Every Client's Needs section of a Business Plan should ask and answer the same questions. For add-on products, existing clients should be interviewed.

Don't shortcut the process. It is necessary to ask and answer all the questions. Organizations are always changing; a small change in the organization may result in a new need or a refocus on existing needs. The main questions that need to be identified in this document are: (1) expected clients demographics, (2) existing client's requirements, (3) future client's requirements, (4) Development and Client Support recommendations.

The following explains how to identify the questions that need to be asked and where to find the information in order to create a Client's Needs section to your Product Business Plan.

Clients Demographics

Knowledge of a client's demographics is necessary in order to identify who will use this product. By creating a generic picture of the typical clients, questions asked in later steps will be easier to answer. The typical questions that may need to be answered are:
- How should this product be visually and verbally presented to the clients?

- What management tools are needed – e.g. what information gathered by the product will management want to see.
- What type of client questions should the Client Support organization handle? The product may be intuitive but will there be communication issues, or issues with employee use? Will Client Support be supporting the product or supporting the use of the product? For example, if the product is credit card processing, will Client Support have to help people process credit cards or will they be dealing with problems that show up on the statement?
- What type, if any, client documentation, will be needed?
- Does the client have access to prerequisite hardware and software? Do they have a Smartphone? Do they need to install security software?

All of the answers generated from this information are instrumental in creating an effective product and an accurate budget.

For example, Executive staff wants specific information from the sales organization. Development was asked to create a report that the branch managers can use to input sales data. By visiting a branch office and seeing how the sales organization currently works it becomes apparent that the sales people are currently gathering the requested information but this information isn't being captured by the current process. Instead of creating an input screen for the sales managers, it would be more effective to update a sales app: where the sales people directly input the information into their phone; the data is saved on the corporate server; and sales management can pull reports.

The aim is to understand who has the data, who uses the data, and who needs the data, to identify what the product and documentation should look like, and what type of client interface is needed. The interface will be different if the product will be accessed by a manager sitting in front of a PC, or a sales person using their Smartphone, or a loading dock worker using a tablet or a shared PC.

Current Client Requirements

Provide detail on why and how the clients are currently working, what they like about their current situation, and what changes and features they would like to see is essential in understanding a future release. If the new product changes the way clients currently work it may be necessary to identify and predict their reaction. A client base that is opposed to change will need more handholding during release. This additional support will need to be built into the cost of the product.

Many times organizations overlook talking to their clients. They believe that they know their clients and have enough client information. In some instances organizations have failed to keep up with clients. If you don't talk to your clients, basic needs may be overlooked and positive features may be designed out.

How to approach the clients: It is necessary to talk directly to clients to get accurate information. Talking to your Client Support organization is another step in creating a Business Plan. Don't shortcut the process. Take the time to talk to clients and the people who support them. The people who use the product are the final judge; they will make or break a product.

The easiest way to talk to clients is through a questionnaire sent via e-mail or placed on the organization's web site. A website questionnaire may be an easy way to get timely feedback from clients. In some situations, you will get better more accurate information by talking to the clients directly by phone or personally visiting them. Many internal clients have opinions they are eager and willing to share about processes that affect them. By going to the source you get timely, accurate information.

Designing a client questionnaire – When designing a questionnaire, start by writing down the information you want answered. Then design the survey questions that will provide you with experiential information. This is harder to do and harder to analyze than a direct question, but the information received will be more accurate. Trial lawyers don't ask prospective jury members if they are prejudiced. They ask them what experiences they have had with a particular group and ask them what they have been told about that group. Experiential questions give better information.

For example, the proposed product is for an authoring tool to create training for the web. The two choices of authoring tools are either hosted on a server or reside on the clients desktop. The goal of your survey is to find out if clients have a preference. A direct question would be, "would you prefer to use an authoring tool that you access over the web or one that resides on your PC?" If your Clients already use a cloud-based app, see if you can ask a question that asks them about their experience. "Have you ever used a cloud-based app like Google office? How does that compare to your experience with Word that resides on your PC?" The second question will give you better feedback.

Filling in the survey: Now that a survey has been created, try it out on someone who matches the client's demographics. Fine tune the questionnaire to make sure the objectives will be met. Take a sample of ten to fifteen current clients and contact them. If they provide similar answers you probably have a good idea regarding their needs. If the answers seem skewed, contact ten more clients. Ten to fifty clients should be all that are needed for most corporate applications. Statistically two thousand responses give you a 97% accuracy rate; this is needed for large consumer focuses surveys like a presidential election, but overkill for most organization's products.

If you're hoping to migrate clients from your website to your mobile app you may want to perform two surveys. One survey can be performed by personally contacting a small group of clients, while the other survey can be placed on your website. Depending on your web traffic, it may be relatively easy to get 2,000 responses from your clients. If you include a free giveaway with the survey, like a T-shirt, you will get a much higher response. You can use the phone call survey as a way to check your Internet survey results.

For large or very important products you may want to create focus groups. In a focus group ask five to ten clients to attend a roundtable meeting. A round table or focus group is just that, a room with a round table where you can bring in a targeted group of people ask them questions, and monitor their response. Since clients may give different answers when in a group, create a set of experiential questions.

One word of warning: don't bias the questions. Don't give the people questioned any more information than they would receive if they were asked to evaluate the product without any access to an organization representative. There are many examples of products that had extensive focus groups that failed. One reason is leading the people in the focus group. In the early 1980's, soon after IBM released the PC, they came out with a "chicklet" keyboard. Focus groups loved the new keyboard but critics slammed it and clients didn't buy chicklet PCs. Upon further study, it was found that focus group leaders trained potential focus group members upfront by extolling the virtues of a chicklet keyboard. The information focus group members received was not the same information provided to the buying public, skewing the results.

New Client Requirements

Smartphone technology is a good example of new technology that may present a different paradigm than expected. You may want to provide a new Smartphone service. For example, a bank may want to include Smartphone access to their clients' accounts. Corporate clients use PC's not Smartphones at work. An app that lets them take a picture of their checks isn't of use since the client isn't accessing their account that way. It might be better to include a web service that lets the client upload a scanned image of a check. Whereas consumers might better use a phone version of that application since consumers may not have a scanner and have a higher likelihood of using a smartphone instead of a computer. Also, consumers who don't have computers, but have Smartphones, may be a new client base for online accounts. Understanding clients' needs will provide a richer, better-focused feature set, and happier clients.

Future Client Requirements

Apply the client's demographics defined earlier in this document to define who the target client is. Future clients may or may not be your existing clients. Who else is your organization looking to support? Using the previous example, the bank had a group of clients who were not using online banking services. With the mobile app, they can now reach these people. What needs do these people have? What limitations do they have – e.g. printing out statements might be a limitation.

Another example is a payroll program. Traditionally clients have been the accounting department. Accounting employees are in an office, sitting in front of a computer – they don't need a mobile app. Whereas a time card mobile app for employees that ties into the payroll program may make employees more efficient and allow managers to be more responsive. With scheduling on their SmartPhone, employees can view their schedule, input their availability, and set reminders so they are not late for work. These employees are not the traditional client but a future client made available through mobile apps.

Development and Client Support Organization

Internal groups live and breathe the product day in and day out. Don't forget to tap these resources. Again create a questionnaire, take the time to ask Client Support people for their opinion. Additionally, you can host an internal roundtable. Make sure you take a sample of employees. Don't always use the same people. Don't always ask the star performers. Some organizations are afraid of asking internal people since they think a roundtable will turn into a gripe session. A session, properly managed, with a set agenda and clear goals will be informative and positive. For an existing product, have Client Support create a "wish list" of features they believe should be in the product. This is a list made up of client requests. A wish list is an excellent foundation for the Product Backlog.

Sales Organization

For external client products, talk to your sales organization. Sales people are intimately aware of what clients want and don't want. Check with a few different sales people to ensure that the information one sales person provides is not skewed to a particular client's situation and that recommendation will provide across the board solutions. Also, don't just ask star performers. Mid-range performers might have a very different client base with very different needs.

Use the Internet

Almost every solution in existence has an Internet chat group. Timely information can be readily accessed on the Internet regarding this solution or market space. The chat groups contain a lot of good market information along with good vendor information. Search under keywords for the solution being developed and hardware and software vendor's names. Other organizations might be developing a similar solution, you can learn from their recommendations.

A caveat to watch out for when creating the Client's Needs section is that when interviewing people, they tend to provide a solution instead of identifying problems and requirements. The Phase 1 Lead will need to identify when a client is providing a solution and not identifying a problem. To make the process effective the Phase 1 Lead should have the clients explain why their proposed solution is better, what problem their proposed solution solves. The real information the Phase 1 Lead is identifying is the problem. Let your Development Team come up with the solution.

The reason the Phase 1 Lead wants to stay away from identifying solutions is clients may be unaware that a better, more cost effective, or simpler solution is available. Additionally, your Development Team may decide to purchase different software or hardware than the one the client recommends. Unbeknownst to your Development Team the new software may not have the features the client really needs. Development's job is to look at requirements and come up with the best solution. The Phase 1 Lead needs to provide them with accurate information so they can make an informed decision.

Product Environment

The Phase 1 Lead should answer deeper questions on the product and it's positioning before they create a Product Backlog.

Scope and Description

For the following, provide one to five sentences for each point. The answers should not be HOW, they should be WHAT e.g. Does the product need documentation: Answer: Yes, Client Support and the client's will need online documentation. Client Support will need to debug errors, Clients will need end user installation documentation. By answering these questions, you'll be providing a snapshot in time for future review.

Product Overview: If this is a new version of an existing product, present only the differentiators between this release and the previous release.

- The Market: What is currently going on in the industry that relates to this product?
- The Competition: Who is the competition, what products complete and does the completion have any winning features?
- Target Clients: Who will use this product, e.g. existing client, same client different client, new client, new markets?
- Product Vision: What is the role of this product? What need will this product fill?
- Product Objectives: How will this product fill the role and need?
- Fit within existing and/or future product line: Where does this product fit into the overall corporate scheme? What are the organization's goals and how does this product meet those goals?
- Market positioning: How does this product support the organization's market vision and direction?

Features:
- Performance Goals: What are the specific performance goals of this product?
- Industry Standards: If applicable provide existing standards organizations and how this product needs to conform.
- Compatible Platforms: What hardware and software platform will this product work on?
- Prerequisites: What prerequisites are necessary for this product to work?
- Scalability: What are the limits to the products growth? Hardware and software that can support 1 to 10,000 clients are considered very scalable. Scalability identifies the ability of a solution to grow from small to large with minimum changes.
- Latency: How fast does the product need to respond.
- Client Support: What training/support will Client Support need to release and support this product?
- Serviceability: What features will be needed to service this product?
- Connectivity: What will this product need to connect to, what conductivity will be needed to support this product?
- Hardware/Software: What additional hardware/software will the organization need to procure to run/support/service this product?
- Client Support Requirements: What requirements will be needed to support the product?
- Documentation Requirements: What internal and client documentation will be needed?
- Beta: Will there be a beta release?
- Key Risks/Open Issues: List risks and open issues that could jeopardize release, costs, and potential revenue.

Product Backlog

The Product Backlog is a living document that is the basis for the technical implementation. Once the product's clients and their needs have been identified a product Story is created. Each Story explains how the product will operate.

It's True: A group of Stories is called an Epic

For example, if the product is a Smartphone CRM application, the Story may be: The sales person receives a notification to contact a client, a button displays to call the client, a note box with client name, company; time, date and the last conversation is displayed.

- Development eventually will turn Stories into Tasks.
- A Product Backlog is a list of Stories.
- These Stories explain product features and functionality, not how to implement the feature.
- The Product Backlog is prioritized from most important to least important Story.
- The prioritized list is divided into at least three sections A, B, & C. "A" lists the features that must be in the product for the product to work, "B" lists the features that would be nice to have, "C" lists the features that would be nice to have, but most clients could live without.
- This is a living document. That is over the life of this product Stories will be added, deleted and reprioritized.

It's True: The Phase 1 Lead creates the Product Backlog.

The Development Lead reviews the Product Backlog, clarifies each Story with the Phase 1 Lead, then provides an estimated timeframe it will take to complete each Story. This is only a gross estimate; Development does not do deep research or prototype the story. Time frames should be in weeks or months. The goal is not to create a project plan. The goal is to identify if the project will take a quarter, a year, or five years to produce.

The example below is for an organization-wide directory app. Each line item is one "Story". The Phase 1 Lead ranks all the Stories from highest to lowest priority, then groups them in an A,B,& C priority. From this Product Backlog, the Development Lead provides a straw man time frame to develop each Story. For this example, all features are in man months.

Rank	Story	Group	Time
1	Create product architecture	A	3M
2	Instant access to employees by name or department, or location	A	1M
3	List of potential employees with partial information	A	1M
4	Integrating features with existing cloud programs	A	2M
5	One button access to text, e-mail	B	1M
6	Available for iPhone clients	B	1M
7	Available for Android clients	B	1M
8	Integration with room scheduling software	C	1M
9	Include picture of employee application	C	1M
10	Access to internal IM application	C	1m

Figure 1-2 Initial Product Backlog

"A" lists the Stories that must be in the product for the product to work, "B" lists the Stories that would be nice to have, "C" lists the Stories that would be nice to have, but most clients could live without. The Developer Lead annotates the list with approximately how long they estimate it to take to develop each Story.

To create a conservative estimate, the lead developer should double the amount of time they think any specific Story will take. This allows vacations, technical debt, bug fixes, and design changes to be factored into development. This document does not reflect an actual schedule, just an estimate used for planning purposes.

The goal of Phase 1 is to identify the scope of the product so that management can make an intelligent decision to fund a product. It is important to note that Development fears this document. Their concern is, they will be held accountable in later stages for estimates provided in Phase 1. For this process to work, it is very important that management realizes that estimates presented in Phase 1 should only be used to decide if a product should be funded. Management will need to let Development scope and design the product before they hold them accountable for their estimates.

Estimating Product Costs

The Phase 1 Lead is responsible for developing the necessary documentation the Executives will need to understand, analyze and approve or deny new product development. The Initiation plan will include:
- Estimated people cost
- Estimated equipment cost
- Estimated time frame

Tip: For a quick cost, estimate 1X for hardware, 2X for software and 3X for people and services e.g. If your hardware costs $50,000 your software will cost $100,000 and your people and support will cost $300,000 a year. Support cost isn't the cost for help desk; it's the behind the scenes cost for managing and maintaining the product.

Developing an Estimated Cost

The Phase 1 Lead has a prioritized Product Backlog that the Development Lead has updated with approximate time frames. This provides an approximate timeframe for the first increment of software to be delivered and ballpark on how long the entire project will take.

Figuring out people costs – The Phase 1 Lead needs to work with their Development Lead to figure out how many developers will be needed based on developing A, B, and C features; is this one team or many team project. Your accounting department should be consulted in order to understand what the fully burdened cost per person in your organization is. A rule of thumb cost is $200,000 per person-year. Add up the number of man-hours, divide by 40 (hours in a week), divided by 52 (weeks in a year). This will give you the approximate cost for developers. For estimated costing, it is not necessary to understand overlaps or pregnant process. At this point only the days or weeks that will be spent developing the product.

Example: Development Lead predicts this project will take 280 man weeks to complete.
Development time will be: 280/52=5.38 man-years
Development cost will be: 5.38 x $200,000= $1,076,000

The Phase 1 Lead should also figure that Development is only 50% of the time and cost it takes to bring a product to completion. If the Development Lead predicts they can complete the product in six months, the Phase 1 Lead should estimate that the product would be available in twelve months, since the remaining 50% of the time it takes to develop a product is to, create documentation, quality assure, beta test, and, if necessary, count for the staging and release of hardware and software. Don't short cut this time. This is your quality time and a product not properly tested is guaranteed to fail. It's ten times more expensive to fix a product once it is in the clients' hands than before it's released.

Example: Based on 5.38 development years
Beta, and staging hours: 5.38 x $200,000 = $1,076,000
People cost for product: = $1,076,000 x 2 = 2,152,000

When estimating a product for budgeting purposes, it is wise to double the cost and round the number.

Estimated people cost for the product: $4,200,000

Many times the Phase 1 Lead knows up front the head count assigned to a product and the date the organization expects the future product to be fully available. Don't plan a preliminary schedule by counting backward. Take the time to review the Development Lead's estimates. If the time frame causes the product to be late, reevaluate the products A, B, and C priorities. If necessary, shuffle the priorities. By changing your prioritization, your new estimate may map better with the company's expectations. Alternatively provide a date for A priority, B priority, and C priority. Present the original scheduled to executive staff and provide the shuffled schedule, explain the pros and cons of choosing each direction.

Identifying equipment costs: Some products require new hardware and software to be purchased. An example would be: updating everyone's Smartphones or providing the sales organization with tablets. Behind the scenes, you may now need new servers to manage the data being served and gathered by the application, along with new database technology and new security applications. Apps are just the front end to large data solutions.

To estimate equipment costs, you will use the same initial documents found in the Business Plan. Don't spend the time now getting bids or identifying specific vendors. Currently, you only need an estimate a general cost. Identify a generic ballpark configuration of hardware that you believe will meet your needs. Find out the cost. Multiply this cost by the number of clients. Estimate that it will cost you twice as much for software as for the hardware. Estimate that it will cost twice as much to install and support the hardware, on a yearly basis than the software cost. Use list prices for the hardware, this will provide you with buffer room.

Example: New Smartphones for employees:
Each iPhone will cost $650
Each iPad will cost $500
Servers to host application data $250,000
Software for servers $500,000

People cost to manage the servers and the applications: $1,000,000

Estimated features and release date: The Product Backlog is used to provide a feature list. From this, an estimate of how long it takes will have been provided. Take the estimate provided by the Development Lead and double it. This doubling should provide you with adequate time to test and roll out the solution.

It's True - The fear of many Phase 1 Leads is that their estimate might be too high in cost and time. Phase 1 estimates give management a ballpark figure. Management always lowers the budget and time. Projects always cost more than what anyone initially thinks.

Estimated Potential Revenue

Estimated revenue is the biggest crystal ball exercise of this Business Plan. If the Business Plan is for a new version of an existing product the estimation is more reasonable. The organization already has current revenue and a knowledge of the percent of the industry revenue they own. This new version will either maintain market share or grow market share. Your Sales organization will give estimated sales estimates for the new version. For new add-on's to existing products Sales too can provide estimates. The products that are the biggest crystal ball are new products for new markets. The best way to create this estimate is to:

1. Identify the market
2. Identify the submarket
3. Identify your estimated market reach
4. Identify your target price

For example, if you have a product for young women who use SmartPhones and use social media the following statistics give you a ballpark of how big the market is:

- US SmartPhone users – 222 million
- Market penetration for people over 18 and under 30 – 98%
- Number of women between the ages of 18 and 24 – 30 million

The next step in creating a revenue estimate is to estimate how much of the market you can reach and how that will be reflected in potential revenue.

- Within one year we should reach 25% of women between the ages of 18 and 24 who use SmartPhones - 13 million potential Clients
- Conservative estimate
  - 2% of clients will purchase 10$ of product a year.
  - Estimated revenue is $26 million in sales.
- Optimistic estimate
  - 10% of clients will purchase 10$ of product a year.
  - Estimated revenue is $130 million in sales

Of course this estimate is predicated on lots of what ifs. But it gives management the potential market size.

Phase 1 – Initiation – Presentation

The Phase 1 Lead should now have the information necessary to create an Initiation presentation to executive staff. An Initiation presentation should be kept simple. Executive management needs information and data so they can understand the general cost and scope of a product in order to fund the product. Information to be presented:
- Resource matrix
- Product's Goals
- Client's Needs
- Product backlog
- Estimated development time
- Estimated development cost
- Estimated availability

Tip: Save all phase reviews in a central repository. This information will be beneficial for new team members and executives to review in later phases.

About the Phase 1 Presentation

Once the Business Plan is complete the Phase 1 Lead presents a Phase 1 Initiation review to executive staff. The Phase 1 Lead should bring a copy of the Business Plan, which includes The Product's Goal, The Resource Matrix, Client's Needs, The Product Backlog, and Estimated Costs and Revenue to the meeting. These documents will be back up for any questions executives have regarding the product's estimates.

The simplest and most effective method of running phase reviews is to create a standard boilerplate presentation that can be filled in by Phase 1 Lead and once this product moves to Phase 2 by the Project Manager. By standardizing each phase presentation, confusion is minimized, the Project Manager and teams understand what will be expected of them, this way information presented will be uniform from product to product. This will allow executive staff to fairly judge which products should be funded. Centrally storing documents presented to executive staff provides future team members a document trail by which they can understand what information went into decisions made before they were involved in the product.

At the end of each phase presentation, the executives will need to sign off on the presentation. This is necessary to confirm that executives actually had access to information presented and have agreed to the conclusion.

It is important to understand the approval and funding process within the organization. Funding for Phase 1 products will depend on organization procedures. Some organizations have Phase 1 presentations provided throughout the year. At the budgeting time, they review the Phase 1 products that have been accepted and decide which get funding. Other organizations have designated funds set aside for starting new projects throughout the year. They can approve and fund a product at presentation time.

The Phase 1 Presentation Includes:

Page 1: Cover Page, this document should be for controlled distribution, list the names of all the people attending and receiving the handout. The cover page should have the product name, the phase, and the date.

Page 2: Agenda: list what will be presented, who will be presenting the item, and time allotted for the presentation. Agenda items for a Phase 1 review may be product introduction, marketing overview, development overview, estimated costs, estimated market size, show estimated revenue, issues, and risks.

Page 3: Provide three to five project goals

Page 5: Provide the resource matrix

Page 4: Identify the client, list three to five needs

Page 6: Provide the top "A" Stories from the Product Backlog

Page 7: Show the estimated development costs, Employee cost, Equipment cost, Development time

Page 8: Itemize all the issues and risks.

Page 9: Executive session:

Recommendations for Management and Team Members

Recommendations for Management

- Don't shortcut the process.
- Don't prejudice the development schedule or release date.
- Don't release information received in a Phase 1 review

- Don't hold the team accountable for times, dates, and costs developed in Phase 1

Recommendations for the Phase 1 Lead
- Design survey questions that ask experiential questions.
- Don't overlook the different needs that future client may have
- Don't get caught up in flushing out the details. This is an exercise to understand product scope
- Don't look at specific vendors solutions – try to understand processes

Detailed Management Recommendations

1. Don't shortcut the process. Make sure due diligence is performed on the product. Allow the Phase 1 Lead to perform a market analysis. The time spent interviewing clients up front can save considerable time and money in development. Business journals are littered with great ideas that failed because a complete market analysis was not performed.

2. Don't prejudice the development schedule or release date by top down proclamations. Allow the Phase 1 Lead and the Development Lead to create an estimate. Executive staff has the tendency to want to "fix" the schedule when it doesn't meet dates they are looking for.

The only way to shorten a development schedule is to put more resources on areas that can be shortened, overlay products where applicable or lower the functionality requirements. There is no other way to shorten a proposed schedule unless you want a fool's schedule; one that looks good on paper but is totally unrealistic. With a fool's schedule, management will feel happy until the product slips and the market window is missed. Spend the time up front fostering the proper behaviors and the product will come out on time and on budget. Schedules that are reworked in executive staff meetings are generally reworked without a true understanding of what is required. Shortening schedules should be delegated to the team, executive staff's role is to approve or disapprove information presented.

3. Don't release information received in a Phase 1 review. Phase 1 information is approximate information. Between Phase 1 and the end of Phase 2 dates and costs may change. An in-depth cost study is not performed during Phase 1. The purpose of Phase 1 is to provide management information to decide if money should be allocated to develop an Initiation.

4. Don't hold the team accountable for times, dates, and costs developed in Phase 1. Many people are afraid to provide an estimate because they are concerned they will be held accountable for oversights once the product is funded. Management needs information in order to make a decision. Understand that costs and schedules might drastically change between Phase 1 and Phase 2. Give the Phase 1 Lead and Development the latitude to come up with estimates in order to provide enough information to make a decision.

Documents Created in Phase 1

By Document

- Creators write down their idea
- Executive team vets ideas and decides which ones should be researched
- Stakeholders are identified, measurable and actionable goals are created
- Phase 1 Lead creates a Business Plan that includes
    - Product Feasibility
    - Product Goals
    - Client needs
    - Product environment
    - Product backlog
    - Estimated costs
    - Estimated Revenue
- Phase 1 review is created and delivered

By Department

Developer Phase 1 – Initiation
- Works with Phase 1 Lead on technical product environment
- Provides time estimates for Product Backlog
- Attends phase review

Phase 1 Lead – Initiation
- Creates Resource Matrix
- Product goals
- Creates Business Plan including:

- Clients interviews, surveys, and roundtables
- Decision maker interviews, surveys, and roundtables (if clients are different from decision maker).
- Industry review – what press and analysts say is important
- Competitive review – what are other organizations in your market doing
- Internal review – what features does IT propose
- Client Support review – what features does Client Support want

• Presents information to Executive staff (Phase 1 Review)

Phase 2 – Planning

Phase 2 Objective

The objective of Phase 2 is to define, architect, prototype, and design a product that satisfies the requirements identified in the Phase 1 Business Plan.
- A Project Manager is appointed.
- In Phase 2, Development assigns an architect(s) to design, architect, and where necessary prototype the product outlined in the Business Plan.
- By the end of Phase 2, the Project Team has been created.
- Members of the Project Team include:
  - Client Support
  - Development Manager (representing the Architect)
  - Documentation Manager
  - Marketing Communications
  - Product Marketing
  - Project Manager
  - QA Manager
  - Training Manger

The Players in Phase 2

Management tasks each department to assign a representative to the Project Team. The following highlights the departmental responsibilities.

Client Support Manager – is responsible for defining, designing, and developing a detailed plan that articulates how their organization will support a product after it's released. The Support Plan defines how Client Support staff will be trained, clients will access help, how bugs will be tracked and fixed after release, the training available to clients, and how updates/fixes will be sent to clients.

Development Manager – representing the Architect who is responsible to design and architect the project and responsible for providing costing information.

Documentation Manger – is the functional area responsible for all internal and client related documentation. The manager attends Project Team meetings, provides a Documentation Plan and costing information.

Marketing Communications – is the functional area responsible for all communications inside and outside of the organization. They develop a Marketing Communications plan and provide costing information, and attend meetings.

Product Marketing – is responsible for product direction, industry analysis, and competitive analysis, understanding the client's needs, and identifying and driving product direction. Product Marketing works with all areas within the organization to make sure the product is focused on the client's needs and is presented in the best possible light. Product Marketing is responsible for assuring the Business Plan is kept current.

Project Manager – is responsible for managing the process, keeps the team focused on the product's goals and confirms that deliverables within each stage of the product lifecycle have been met. The Project Manager facilitates communications between team members and among departments. When deliverables slip it is the responsibility of the Project Manager to escalate this information and to facilitate resolution. In smaller organizations, the Product Manager's duties usually incorporate those of Product Marketing and Marketing Communications.

Quality Assurance Manager - is the functional area responsible for assuring products meet corporate quality and the definition of Done. The manager attends Project Team meetings, provides a QA Plan and costing information.

Training Manger – produces any classroom or online training needed for the product. The manager attends Project Team meetings, provides a Training Plan and costing information.

The Planning Phase

Phase 2 starts when the product is funded.
- Product design and architecture including system integration and security is performed.
- Hardware and software are defined and if appropriate ordered.
- The team is formed from members (typically management) of individual departments
- The business plan is reviewed and updated.

The Project Manager works with executives who funded the product, to assure that each of the core functional areas assigns a member to the team. This member is the point person; they represent their function or department. It is the responsibility of the Project Team to provide their functional area with documents, updates, and issues presented in the team meeting. They, in turn, provide the team with documents, updates, and issues from their organization. If a functional area cannot make their product dates, it is the team member's responsibility to notify the Project Manager that there is a problem before the date slips. The Project Manager's responsibility is to understand where there are slippages and come up with a plan that minimizes the effect of any slippage before this issue becomes critical.

As soon as the team is formed, each team member receives a copy of the Business Plan created in Phase 1. From this document, they begin to scope out what will be required from their organization to make this product a success.

Creating a Team

To have an effective Project Team, it is necessary to create a group of people who can work with each other.

- Inherent in a team's dynamics are members who bring opposing interests and hidden agendas.
- It is the responsibility and goal of the Project Manager to create a functioning group of people.
- Creating a team is one of the most difficult, but important responsibilities the Project Manager has.

Project Teams that start from the rockiest beginning many times turn out to be the most effective teams. Team members who really care about the quality of the product early on create much of the disagreements and hostility displayed at team meetings. The disagreements are their way of making their department's goals understood. This negative energy can be used to create an effective team. It is the mission of the Project Manager to focus and channel this energy.

There are five stages in creating a team. The first four stages of team growth were first developed by Bruce Wayne Tuckman and published in 1965. His theory, called "Tuckman's Stages" was based on research he conducted on team dynamics. He believed that the five stages are inevitable for a team to grow to the point where they are functioning effectively together and delivering high-quality results.

Stage 1: Forming – clear goals need to be presented

Stage 2: Storing – the team members compete with each other for status and for acceptance of their ideas

Stage 3: Norming – focused on developing a way of working together

Stage 4: Performing – functioning at a very high level

Stage 5: Adjourning – celebrate the success of the project and capture best practices for future use

Getting Started:

Ground Rules: The first step in creating an effective team is to clearly lay down ground rules. It is a good idea to create a list of ground rules at the first team meeting.

An example of a list of ground rules is:
- All members are responsible for showing up on time with assignments complete.
- If a team member has not completed a task assigned to them it is their responsibility to notify the Project Manager before the meeting.
- All discussions will remain professional; all comments must be focused on tasks, not people. No slander, swearing or personal insults are allowed.
- The Project Manager has complete authority for maintaining order.
- The Project Manager can interrupt any team member at any time and ask them to shorten their comments or handle their discussion out of the meeting.
- It is the responsibility of the Project Manager to decide what conversations are pertinent to the team.
- Not all discussions are pertinent to all team members all the time. Team members should show curtsey to each other by allowing members of the team the time to discuss their issues even when it does not involve everyone.
- Team members who break any team rules owe the entire team an apology.

After the guidelines of conduct are discussed and agreed to it is recommended that all team members sign the bottom of the ground rules sheet agreeing to follow the rules of the team. Some teams find that financial incentives help keep team rules in check. With some teams, a penalty box should be instituted. If team members are late to meetings and have not called ahead to notify the project manager of their conflict they have to pay $1 a minute for each minute they are late. If they come unprepared they have to pay $1 to $5. This money goes into the penalty box. Team members modify their behavior quickly after they are forced to pay money. It's a good idea to keep a running total of penalty box money in the team minutes. When the funds hit a pre-defined number or date the team gets lunch or a cake (depending on how much penalty box money there is).

Team Goal: It is important to clearly state the goal of the team. This provides clarity and purpose for the team. Use the goals created in Phase 1. The goals can be used as a benchmark to decide what is important and what is pertinent to the team. It keeps the team focused on the big picture. Goals can be used as a bi-line for the team minutes.

Identifying hidden positions: A Project Manager needs to understand and manage the three different types of people that are part of a newly forming team. Supporters, Naysayers and organizational anarchists. Be careful labeling team members, "you can't always judge the book by its cover". Many people appear to be in one category but are actually in another category. Also, people change categories. Your goal is to move your team to the Supporter category.

Supporters – Supporters have typically been involved in teams that have an organized product life cycle. They have learned that a structured approach to product development actually saves time and causes less confusion.

Naysayers – New teams have many naysayers. Naysayers complain that the Waterfall process is bureaucratic, the organization is too small, or the product is too small for a Waterfall process. Do not become intimidated by naysayers, Effective product development needs planning. Many naysayers are actually concerned that the Waterfall process will add unnecessary paperwork to their already overburdened workload. They may be concerned that the Waterfall process will provide their management with a scorecard used to "beat them up" if they slip up. When a Project Manager effectively runs a team a naysayer learns first hand that the team will support them and that an organized approach is easy and more efficient. In the long run, a Waterfall process saves team members time and makes them look good within the organization. Most naysayers turn into the biggest Supporter once they have been involved in an effective team.

Organizational Anarchists – The most difficult group for a Project Manager to identify and deal with are organizational anarchists. Organizational anarchists sound like naysayers or Supporters but are in fact people who are incapable of working within the structure. They are incapable of creating, providing, or working with the necessary paperwork an effective team needs. Most organizational anarchists are nice, interesting, creative people. Most organizational anarchists have been successful individual contributors who feel it is important for their career growth to get into a management track. An organizational anarchist will unknowingly undermine the effectiveness of a team. Once identified, a Project Manager has one of three choices to deal with an organizational anarchist:
1) Replace them
2) Marginalize them
3) Limit their effect

Many times it is difficult for a Project Manager to replace a person assigned to a team. Team members and management might not understand why the Project Manager is trying to get rid of this team member. Getting rid of a team member is a very tricky situation since it can cause a negative team backlash. You should handle this situation carefully.

A successful strategy for dealing with an organizational anarchist is to talk directly with them about their role in the team. They typically feel uncomfortable and overwhelmed by their team role. Saving face makes them want to stay on the team. Help them decide to do what makes them feel comfortable. If they stay, a Project Manager will need to set him/herself up as a coach. This way the Project Manager can marginalize the organizational anarchist's effect. By marginalizing someone, a Project Manager will keep an organizational anarchist on the team but will find other people to help fulfill their duties. Sometimes a substitute person can be found to perform their duties. If all else fails and a Project Manager is forced to work with organizational anarchists the Project Manager must understand any duties that the organizational anarchists is involved in will be considered high risk. The Project Manager will not be able to bring the product in time and on budget during the organizational anarchist high-risk activities. The team behavior will have to be modified so the team can react to the organizational anarchist's limitations.

Creating and fostering trust: Trust is necessary for a team to work efficiently. When watching a winning sports team, it is obvious when teammates trust one-an-other by the way they intuitively work with each other. A player on a successful team who trusts their fellow team members will act accordingly. Trust, is not given lightly, it must be earned. A Project Manager builds and creates an atmosphere of trust. The Project Manager provides cues to the team on proper behavior.

To create trust, it is necessary for the Project Manager to be above board with the team. A Project Manager cannot take sides. They must act as a judge, listening and viewing all sides and points of view. Decisions are made based on the project's goals. A Project Manager needs to provide an atmosphere where team members can raise problems and concerns without being labeled a complainer or troublemaker. The Project Manager needs to maintain team member's confidences. When an issues or concern is raised a Project Manager needs to investigate all sides and arbitrate a solution. Team members will want the Project Manager to be their advocate. It is necessary for the Project Manager to be an impartial team advocate. This is accomplished by staying focused on the team's goal. Team members will recognize if a team leader is impartial and focused on the greater good. This will foster trust. When team members trust a Product Manager, team members will provide the Project Manager with crucial information that identifies potential problems before they become fires; thus creating an effective and efficient team.

Effective Styles: Many new Product Managers look at an established Project Manager and attempt to mimic their style. This can easily come off as insincere. The best advice to a new Project Manager is to be yourself. A successful Project Manager can have any personal style. There are specific behaviors that all good Project Managers share. The best Product Managers are organized, fair, support their team, and follow a predictable course like the procedures outlined in this book.

Creating Team Minutes

It is good policy to use a standard template for team minutes and update team minutes after every meeting.
- It is a good idea to maintain items on the team minutes until they are crossed off. This way there is an audit trail of what has been communicated and agreed.
- Team members are responsible for reading the team minutes and getting back to the Project Manager if they don't agree with something written in the team minutes.
- A standard Team Minutes which is updated within a day of a team meeting is a good method for Project Manager to keep track of details and ensures that team members and executives are aware of team issues.

Project Team Attendance:

Responsibility/Name:	Date	Date	Date	Date	Date	Date
Architect						
Client Support						
Communications						
Product Marketing						
Product Owner						
Project Manager						
Scrum Master						

Priority issues:

Executive actions:

Team Issues:

Status by Department:
Architect:
Client Support:
Communications:
Product Marketing:
Product Owner:
Project Manager:
Scrum Master:

Figure 2-1 Sample Team Minutes

Development's Role in Phase 2

After the team members are assigned, the Project Manager reviews with each member their role, responsibility and Phase 2 deliverables. The critical path member of Phase 2 is Development. Development is responsible for:
- Reviewing the estimates created in Phase 1 and the Product Backlog.
- Performing an in-depth review, design, prototype, and architecture for the project.

Development is not creating the product. They are developing a higher level design for the product. Depending on the complexity of the product, a design and architecture may take as short as a week to many months. This may include creating prototypes to assure feasibility of the design.

- The Product Backlog created in Phase 1 is used as the basis for the design document.
- Presenting the minimal requirements for an appropriate design document and identifying what issues are crucial to the product's design.
- Creating a good design

Development has the central role in Phase 2– Planning. The design of any product is the foundation of the product. A bad design will produce a solution that will not meet the needs of the organization. The product design most likely will include creating a design for each of the elements within this project:

It's True: People unfamiliar with developing products don't necessarily understand the need for design. They don't understand why the process takes so long and why Development can't create a solution faster. Fifty percent of the time it takes to develop a product is typically taken in the design stage.

One analogy is building a house. In Initiation, you decide what features you want in a house and figure out your budget. In Planning, you hire an architect to create your blueprints. In Development you build the house.

A new solution that will need to access the company's database might look easy to create but may take months to design. The last thing an organization wants is a messed up database. Data integrity is foremost to any organizations survival. A slight error can erase a sale, or provide a hole that a hacker can use to steal organization records. Planning gives Development time to ensure that the information is gathered in a safe manner that won't affect other applications or corrupt the database.

Planning is when a deep understanding of the product's requirements is undertaken and a plan for developing a solution is created. The design does not include programming or purchasing equipment. The person(s) responsible for design will need to identify minimal and optimal requirements and crucial issues. Many times prototypes will be created in Planning so that the designer can assure that their ideas are workable. Never confuse prototypes with development. The goal is to assure the idea works, it is not to develop a working solution. In most organizations, a senior developer or architect actually creates the design.

Creating a Good Design – Design is the most important step in developing any solution. It is important to take the time upfront to develop a successful design. Here are some standard, logical steps that if followed will ensure a successful design.

1. Great designs don't come from committees they come from great designers. It is impossible for multiple people to create a good design. Designate one senior person to design the product, the design team may consist of a manager who will go to meetings, a "designer in training" to assist the designer, a person responsible for documenting the design, and a person responsible for developing design tests.
2. Clearly, understand what the short and long term goals might be for this product. A good design allows for future growth.
3. View the design from many angles. If all the constraints were removed would the design be different? If so, it is beneficial to re-evaluate the design. For example: during the heat of the space race in the 1960s, the U.S. National Aeronautics and Space Administration decided it needed a ball-point pen to write in the zero gravity confines of its space capsules. After considerable research and development, the astronaut pen was developed at a cost of $1 million. The pen worked and also enjoyed some modest success as a novelty item back here on Earth. The Soviet Union, faced with the same problem, used a pencil.
4. Designing should be an interactive process. Designers should continually test their design theory. A practice that will lead to a good design is to, design, test, design test...
5. Aim for a clean, simple design. If the design is too difficult or to "brilliant" it will be difficult to develop and debug the product. When the product goes to clients, bugs may be difficult to identify and fix.

The Design Review

After the product has been designed an experienced person or a panel of experienced people should review the design.

- A design review confirms that the product's design is, reasonable, obtainable, efficient and realistic.
- A design review affords the architect a forum whereby objective professional reviews the product design to assure it is appropriate before the application is created or hardware and software are ordered.
- Design reviews goal is to catch errors up front which will save money in the long run.

When Development finishes designing the product it is necessary to have a Development design review. A design review is conducted in front of a panel of senior members of the company's Development staff or an outside consultant is brought in. Design reviews confirm that the product's design is, reasonable, obtainable, efficient and realistic. If the organization is small or all the expertise in that particular area was used to design the document it is recommended that an outside expert(s) who has yet to see the design be brought in to review the product's design.

Many products hit snags in Scrum, Beta, and after they are released because there was not a planned opportunity for an objective professional review of the design document and to confirm that the design was appropriate before Scrum-Development began. Many times the process of the design review makes the designer do their homework and ensure that all considerations have been met. No matter what the size of the organization, a design flaw found up front saves money down the line.

Guidelines need to be developed in order to have successful design reviews. Some designers are threatened by design reviews. A designer may have spent up to a year designing a product. They may resent an outsider review what they have done. Don't let this resistance stop the organization from reviewing the design. Don't let a designer's status cause you to waive this requirement. An experienced designer can still overlook things. To make design reviews a positive experience the following is recommended:

- Apply design reviews to everyone. Singling out designers or Development groups creates bad feelings.
- Provide the designers with a list of what will be looked for up front. This helps the review panel and the designers being reviewed
- Review with the designers and the review panel the purpose of this review.
- Provide a neutral facilitator
- Make this an enjoyable process. A designer can show that they are senior by coming in with a well thought out complete design.

It is necessary for Development to identify up front what the review panel will look for. For instance, if the product is responsible for developing a hardware solution the design panel will be told to look for solutions that use easily found parts. The designers will know they will be asked to justify the parts they have chosen. If a piece of hardware needs to be specially ordered or the part has been announced but is not currently on the market the review committee will know this product's success is high risk and may ask the designer to identify a different solution. The designers will know up front what questions will be asked. Anticipating these questions will provide the designer with the time to identify how to defending their design ideas and will make them accountable for doing their homework up front.

Team Member's – What Everyone Else Is Doing.

While Development has the critical path responsibilities. The rest of the team receives the Business Plan and the Design Document. From this, they create plans that identify the scope and detail of what their department will be creating. After the Design Review, the design document is shared with the team. The architect is made available to meet with the team so that they can ask questions to better understand the product. Product Marketing is also available to review general scope of the product and the Product Backlog.

Members of the product team
- Client Support
- Development Manager
- Documentation Manager
- Marketing Communications
- Product Marketing
- Project Manager
- Quality Assurance Manager
- Training Manager

Client Support reviews the Business Plan and the Design Document to identify what they anticipate their people will need to support Clients. Then they identify what will be needed in their department in order to learn, support, and identify problems once the product is released. Client Support needs to review the design document and documentation to assure that features their department needs will be tested the way they perceive them to be used. They work with Documentation to outline what they expect to be available so that Clients can install, understand, and use the product by themselves.

The easier the product is to install and use the more independent the Client is. An independent Client saves the organization money in the long run since they use fewer resources than a dependent client. It is worthwhile to put time and energy up front while developing the product to create a product that will be easily supported once released.

Client Support – should be aware of the cost advantage of developing a product that allows clients independence. They are the team member responsible for championing easy to use features – that is clear information that is easy to access regarding the use of the product. Client Support needs to review their organization's ability to service the product and identify what changes are needed to make the organization more efficient, so they can provide better support.

Development - The Development Manager creates a plan by identifying the number of developers needed to develop the product, the skill sets of people currently in their group, and identify what training or additional head count they will need.

Documentation – At this stage, the Documentation Manager reviews the Design Document and Business Plan to identify the type of documentation that should be created and departmental budget for the resources needed. From this information, they create a Documentation Plan.

Marketing Communications – Reviews the Business plan. Once the product starts rolling out communications will need to be promoting the product. At this point, they plan for this accordance by identifying what type of PR, Advertising, articles, and promotions will be created around the product and how often these promotions will run. This information is identified in a Communications Plan. Associated with this plan is a budget that identifies the cost of executing this plan.

Product Marketing – reviews and updates the Business Plan, creates a Launch Plan and Supports Marketing Communications as they create the Communications Plan. The Launch Plan identifies the material they will develop for Sales (presentations), collateral (brochures, white papers, website updates, customer stories) presentations at conferences, and customer tours.

Project Manager – After the Design Review, Development should have a concrete plan defining what will be created, when it will be created, how long it should take to create each Story, and the Product's hardware and software needs. After the Design Document is completed the Project Team receives this document and creates a plan for their department. Once all the plans are created they can create an Integrated Schedule and the Base Line Cost Document.

Roll Out Plan

If the project includes the roll out of 3rd party hardware, software, and networking equipment, the Project Manager will be responsible to create a plan for the purchase and roll out of this equipment. The Roll Out Plan includes targets for receiving, staging, and installing the equipment along with targets of when vendors need to be chosen and estimated ship dates. In Phase 3, the Project Manager, and Development Manager will review different vendor's solutions, negotiate price, and identify the delivery schedule. After contracts are signed they will update the Roll Out plan with vendor details.

Quality Assurance – reviews the Design Document and Business Plan and creates a plan for quality assurance. Once development begins the person responsible for creating the documentation will be part of the cross function Development Team.

Training – reviews the Design Document and Business Plan and creates a Training Plan.

Updating the Product Backlog

After the Architect completes the product design, the Product Backlog is updated by the Product Manager
- Each Story in the Product Backlog is reviewed to assure it is still relevant and new Stories haven't emerged or market conditions haven't changed the priority.
- All Stories are prioritized based on clients' needs and organization direction and then cataloged as A, B, & C priority.
- The updated document will be used by the Project Team and the Scrum Team.

The Product Backlog was initially created in Phase 1 – Concept by the Phase 1 Lead. Starting in Phase 2 the Product Manager takes over the responsibility of updating the Business Plan including being responsible for the Product Backlog. The Product Backlog is updated so that it reflects any changes in the market or organizational priorities. All Stories in the Product Backlog are prioritized and given an A, B, or C status. "A" lists the features that must be in the product for the product to work; "B" lists the features that would be good to have; "C" lists the features that would be interesting to have but are not necessary.

In Phase 1 – Concept the Developer Lead reviewed the Business Plan and made a guess at what it would take to execute the product. This guess was used to identify the general scope and cost of the product. In Design, the product is studied in depth. The estimated developed in Phase 1 are now replaced with actual predictions identified by the rigorous design.

Product Flow from Development through Release:

The flow of deliverables through development, beta, and release including hand-offs and deliverables will be created.
- Acceptance criteria for the definition of Done
- Acceptance criteria to move a product from increment to Beta is created.

Figure 2-2 Integrating the Project Team with the Scrum Team

Development Flow

Starting in Phase 3 there will be two teams running parallel: the Project Team and the Scrum Team. The Scrum Team is a cross-functional Development Team of three to nine people, the Scrum Master, and the Product Owner.

Each development increment is called a Sprint. At the beginning of each Sprint, the Product Owner meets with the Development Team for a Sprint Planning meeting. The Sprint Team decides on a Sprint Goal, breaks Product Backlog Stories down into Tasks, chooses the number of Tasks from the top of the Product Backlog that they believe they can finish within the Sprint, and agrees on a definition of Done for the chosen Tasks. After a pre-determined timebox, the Sprint ends and the increment is presented at a Sprint Review.

The Project Team is invited to attend the Sprint Review. After the Sprint Review, the Project Team decides if the Sprint increment will be released. The Project Team will need to create a process to take increments and turn them into released products.

The cycle of Story-to-Task-to-increment repeats for each Sprint. The Project Team creates a process whereby increments are moved from increment-to- Beta-to-Availability. After the Sprint Review, the Project Team decides if the increment just completed will be released. If so, the team continues with enacting Phase 4 – Beta.

Acceptance criteria: Two acceptance criteria need to be created by the Project Team: They are the definition of Done, and what it takes to move an increment to Beta.

The Definition of Done

In the Sprint Planning session the Development Team decides with the Product Owner what the definition of Done is for each increment. This definition of Done is based on acceptance criteria provided by the Project Team. This acceptance criterion is not based on specifics for each Task in development, it is a measurement. For example, the Project Team may provide the following definition: Each increment must pass testing and QA based on the QA department's definition of passing outlined in the QA Plan, Documentation must meet Document department's quality standard as outlined in the Documentation Plan. All increments that are Done but lack necessary integration, need to be re-entered into the Product Backlog. They are flagged "Done Increment waiting for Integration." This way the increment has visibility and can be prioritized.

Moving an increment to Beta:

The Project Team creates an acceptance criteria to identify if a Done increment should be moved to Beta or if the increment is placed back in the Product Backlog as it waits for integration or for the rest of the Story to be completed. For example, the Project Team can define that only full Stories are moved to Beta. Or they may group a number of Stories together. This grouping is referred to as an Epic. The Product Team may identify the Epics that will be released.

Creating the Integrated Schedule

An integrated schedule can be created once all the Project Team members review the Design Document and the Product Backlog. Team members use this information to create their department's report for their deliverables.

- An integrated schedule is the core of a successful team. It identifies process and interaction.
- To get departmental buy-in, it is best to create an integrated schedule as a team activity.

One commonly used method to create an integrated schedule is to have each team member provide the Project Manager with their issues, requirements, departmental schedule and preferred flow of information. The Project Manager inputs this information into a product-scheduling program and then produces the integrated schedule.

If a Project Manager creates an integrated schedule without an interactive forum there is no departmental buy-in, opportunity to examine disconnects, and team understanding of handoffs and prerequisites.

A Better Way:

A better method to create an integrated schedule is for the Project Manager to facilitate an interactive forum where each member of the Project Team presents their deliverables and their prerequisites. In an interactive forum, it becomes intuitively obvious where there are disconnecting schedules. An interactive forum usually consists of a half or full day session.

To create a forum the Project Manager has each department break their deliverables down by phase. Each deliverable has an end date, begin date or both. Departmental representatives put all their deliverables up on the board. They then identify what deliverables are prerequisites to their deliverables. This information can now generate an integrated schedule. An integrated schedule is a tool that can be used for correctly setting the level of expectation of product development, identifying an accurate release date, identifying critical path deliverables, identifying departments prerequisites, understanding where schedule slips can or will occur and monitoring the progress of the product through its life cycle.

Running the Session:

The Project Manager asks a representative from each department to break deliverables down by individual action items.

> *TIP: Write each deliverable on a Post –It since they can easily be moved.*

Figure 2-3 Post-It

In the center of the Post-It have each team member identify their activity.

On the right-hand corner of the post, the team member writes the number of days needed to complete this activity – not how long it will take – but elapsed days. Make sure to tell the team members to be conservative with how long it will take them to create their deliverable. Holidays and vacations will need to be taken into account. They will never be given more time then now to create a deliverable.

Give each Post-It a unique number e.g. Development's numbers all start with 9, Quality Assurances numbers all start with 8. Have team members place the department number in the left-hand corner of the Post-It.

Pregnant Processes – A pregnant process is a process that cannot be shortened. That is you cannot add people or time to shorten the time it will take. e.g. you can't get three women pregnant and get a baby in three months. Team members should identify any processes that are pregnant.

The easiest way to do this exercise is to cover a blank wall with Flipchart paper or blank newsprint. At the top of the paper write in months so that Product Team members can place their Post-It's on a wall in chronological order.

After everyone places their Post-It's on the wall have the team members find any prerequisite Post-It activities. Have them place the prerequisite number in the lower right-hand corner of their Post-It. Disconnects between departments will become immediately evident. Team members will begin discussing things like, "if you won't have your action items complete until June I will not be able to start my action item until July. I was planning on starting my action items in May. I guess I need to update my plans." This activity forces communication between team members. This level of communications creates a strong team. Team members begin to understand interactions and negotiate solutions with each other. For example team members may say, "If I break this deliverable into two stages I can give you what you need earlier so your deliverables can be available on time".

If the Project Manager creates a schedule without team interaction these negotiations do not take place until there is a crisis. Schedules created using the interactive forum method tend to be extremely accurate since team members will discuss prerequisites.

The team has now created a paper integrated pert schedule for the product. The Project Manager can roll up all the paper and use it to create a computer version of this pert chart. This integrated schedule is a tool that can be used to correctly set the level of expectation of product development, identify an accurate release date, identify critical path deliverables, identify department's prerequisites, understand where schedule slips can or will occur, and be used to monitor the progress of the product through its life cycle.

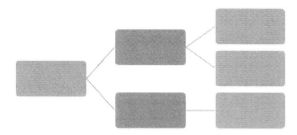

Figure 2-4 Post-It Exercise Pert Chart

TIP: One common mistake when creating an integrated schedule is for the team to be told when deliverables must be completed. Don't succumb to a top-down delivery schedule. Allow the team to build an integrated schedule organically – based on how long tasks will actually take.

If the schedule doesn't meet a hard date handed down by management, a realistic schedule will be needed so that the team can figure out realistic changes. There are many actions a team can take to shorten the release time without misrepresenting the time it takes to accurately complete a task. The team can better assess risk when they start from a realistic schedule. The team can identify what tasks may be performed simultaneously or earlier, where extra resources can be added to minimize time, and what features if minimized, will decrease release time. Since the team is taking the initiative, this is a bottom-up process.

After a realistic integrated schedule is created, team members provide their estimated budget to the Project Manger so a baseline cost document can be created.

Managing Change:

An effective Project Managers properly manages management's expectations. That is they understand what management wants, specifically why a specific date was handed down to the team. They also provide management with information so informed decisions can be made.

There are three fixed elements to any project – Time – Features – Money. A team can spend more time to get the features they need, lessen the features to get the product out on time, or with more money hire, outsource, or purchase what they need to shorten the process.

When the integrated schedule does not meet the schedule handed to the Project Manager the first thing they should do is to go back to the Project Team and ask them the following two questions:
- What features can you cut to pull the schedule back so we can make the delivery?
- What money (to hire new people, outsource, or purchase what's necessary) do you need to get the product out earlier?

For example, an app that provides driver location for deliveries is being developed. The organization will be creating an iPhone and Android version of the app. This app directly interfaces with a GPS system that the company has attached to each of its trucks. If this product schedule identifies its availability will be past the due date management sets, the team can choose one of the following:

1. Feature solution – Make the iPhone app available now with the Android app available at a future date. And/or list the features that will be available with the first release and provide a timetable with features for future releases.
2. Time Solution – Provide a new date the fully featured project will be available
3. Money Solution – Present to management that for an additional amount the project will be on time and fully functional. A possible money solution is to propose that two or more Development Teams are simultaneously working on the solution.

Creating a Base Line Cost Document

The baseline cost document provides an accurate picture of the real cost of developing the product. Each department representative on the Project Team provides the Project Manager with their costing information. This information is now rolled up into a Base Line Cost Document. This document is the realistic version of the Estimated Product Cost created in Phase 1 of the Business Plan.

The four subcategories of costs found in this document include:
- Staffing
- External and internal capital requirements
- Material requirements
- other direct costs

> *It's True: The Base Line Cost Document does not include sustaining costs. The sustaining cost will be developed in Phase 3.*

The Project Manager creates a Baseline Cost Document. This document is used to itemize all costs attributed to this product. The Baseline Cost Document provides executive staff an accurate picture of the real cost of the product along with providing accurate detail for creating accounting documents. There are four subcategories of costs that each department needs to provide to the Product Manager: staffing, external and internal capital requirements, material requirements, and other direct costs. The Project Manager needs to work with each of the Project Team members to get their department's costs so that the document can be completed.

Project:
Organization:
Prepared by:

PRODUCT LIFE CYCLE
DEVELOPMENT COST BASELINE
STAFFING REQUIREMENTS
(Man months per Quarter)

Item #	Labor Type	Task Description	Name	FY Plan (Yes/No)	Q1	Q2	Q3	Q4

Figure 2-5 Staffing Requirements

Staffing Requirements – Each department needs to provide the Project Manager with information on that department's staffing requirements. Staffing requirements detail information on the number of employee hours it will take to produce this product. The information necessary to identify is: the employee status (consultant, part-time, full-time, or exempt), the employee's department and position (i.e.: engineer, database manager, GUI designer), name of each employee, if this person is included within the department's existing fiscal plan and a number of hours this employee will be working on this product by quarter.

Project name: Product life Cycle

Organization:　　　　　　　Development Cost Baseline
Prepared by:　　　　　　　　Capital Requirements

Item #	Description	Qty.	Program Usage (%)	Usage Start Date (mm/yy)	As set #	Existing AcqDate (Qtr/FY)	Price	New Acq. Date (Qtr/FY)	Unit Price	Usage End Date

Figure 2-6 Capital Requirements

External and Internal Capital Requirements – Most projects require the purchase of additional equipment and the amortization of equipment associated with the product. The Capital Requirements document provides detail on capital and equipment either developed internally or purchased. It is necessary for each department to identify: the capital item, the percent this program will use this resource, if the organization will capitalize the equipment, date the department will begin to use the item, capital identifying number the organization assigned to this equipment, date the product was acquired, cost of purchasing components or internal cost of capital, and date the program will stop using this equipment. For capital-intensive products e.g. replacing all employees' PC's, an estimate of cost will need to be used. Negotiations for new equipment will take over the course of place in Phase 3.

Project name:　　　　　　　Product Life Cycle
Organization:　　　　　　　Development Cost Baseline
Prepared by:　　　　　　　Material Requirements

Item #	Description	Purchase Date (Qtr/FY)	Unit of Measurement	Qty	Unit Price	Total Price

Figure 2-7 Material Requirements

Material Requirements – Material requirements details information on the cost of purchasing materials that are under $1,000 and have a useful life of fewer than two years – for example iPhone, iPad and Android's used for development. It is necessary to identify each line item by the department; the date the organization took possession of the materials, the standard unit of measurement, quantity purchased, the price for each unit, and total price.

Project name: Product Life Cycle
Organization: Development Cost Baseline
Prepared by: Other Direct Cost Requirements

Item #	Company Name	Task Description	Period of Service	Estimated Total Price

Figure 2-8 Other Direct Cost Requirements

Other Direct Cost – Other direct costs are items not detailed in the previous sections. Items such as hiring a public relations firm and advertising fall under this category. Identify the name of the organization, the item or service that is being purchased from this organization; describe how the item or service will be used, the length of time this item or service will be used, and the estimated price of this item or service.

Outsourcing

Outsourcing is very popular for development since an organization won't need to hire, train or employ people with the necessary skills. A common mistake is to outsource too early in the process. The issue with outsourcing early is the organization doesn't have a clear idea what the solution or deliverables are. They have yet to do a Cost/Benefit analysis to truly understand the cost of developing the product and hosting the solution.

Organizations that outsource before the end of Phase 2 usually get solutions that don't meet their needs. This is because the organization is not invested in the decision-making process. An outside agency doesn't understand your business the way you know your business. If an organization wants the product to meet their needs they need to clearly define their needs.

After Development creates a Design Document and the Product Backlog is updated, an informed decision can be made. At this point, the organization can interview vendors to see if they can produce a solution that will meet their needs. The Product Manager has created a detailed cost analysis and knows the internal cost of building and hosting the solution. This is powerful information when deciding if it is cost effective to build internally or hire an outside company.

Cost is not the only consideration; control is also a very big consideration. Control is an organizational decision. The importance or proprietary nature of the project may drive the solution to be managed internally.

Some aspects of a solution can be outsourced. For example, the Development or Marketing organization may have web designers but no mobile designers. The cost of sending people to training and the organizational learning curve may be cost and time prohibitive. Hiring an experienced app designer on a contract basis might be the best solution.

Phase 2– Planning – Presentation

At the end of each phase, the Project Manager should have each of the participating team members sign off that they agree their deliverables are complete for that phase. This document provides team members with a sense of control; it builds team unity and assures that representatives take responsibility for their deliverables.

It is helpful for an organization to provide a standard boilerplate presentation that can be modified for each product. This saves the Project Manager time since they will know what will be expected of them. It is also much easier for executives to review products when they are all presented in the same manner. Many times projects can last years and may have more than one Project Manager. A new Project Manager can come up to speed faster if the organization standardizes and catalogs previous presentations allowing new members to come up to speed by understanding the rationale behind decisions.

Sample Phase 2 Presentation Outline:

Page 1: Cover Page. This document should be for controlled distribution. List the names of all the people attending and receiving the review handout. The cover page should have the product name, the phase, and the date.

Page 2: Agenda. List what each team member will be presenting along with the time allotted. Agenda items for a Phase 2 review may include: Introduction, general program status, design review status, team overview, issues, and risks.

Page 3: Planning Phase 2: Review the items that have been created or completed in a Phase 2 Planning:
- Team established
- Product Backlog updated
- Design/architecture created
- Design review completed
- Project Team members each create a plan for their department
- Integrated product schedule created
- Overall costs are identified in a Baseline Cost Document

Page 4: Last phase review action item status -- list action and current status. After the last review, executive staff may have requested action items take place. List those action items along with the status of that item.

Page 5: Integrated schedule: Provide flow and hand-off's

Page 6: Updated costs

Page 7: Each team member gets a page with the highlight of their department's plan

Page 8: Issues and Risks for this Phase: List issue, owner, risk, impact, and status.

Page 9: Executive Session: Executive sign off, Executives note any action items for the team and agree to let the program move to the next phase.

Recommendations for Management and Team Members

Management can support a team by following these guidelines:
- Don't short cut the Waterfall/Scrum process, let the Team define the product and the development schedule
- Respect the development schedule
- Empower the team. Don't give responsibility without authority
- Facilitate information flow
- Take phase reviews seriously
- Make sure design reviews take place

Here are some hints that will help create a successful Project Team:
- Bring in an expert to review the design document.
- Allow the team to build an integrated schedule based on how long they think tasks will take.
- Provide the team members with a forum where they can input and recommend changes if the integrated schedule needs to be modified.

The following are guidelines that executive staff should use to empower the team and assure products come out on time and on budget.

1. Allow the Project Manager and the Team to define the product and the development schedule, don't shortcut the Waterfall/Scrum process.

Business requirements sometimes require a product to be defined and available before Phase 1 or Phase 2 are complete. Don't succumb to allowing outside sources to define your release date and feature list. If you do, the release date you give will slip and the features will not meet expectations or will not be competitive. Phase 1 and 2 are instrumental steps in defining a product. A house built on a bad or non-existing foundation will not weather a storm.

2. Empower the team. Don't give responsibility without authority

Don't send people to the team who do not have the ability to drive process and direction within their group.

4. Facilitate information flow

If contracts are being negotiated outside of the team make sure you provide information access to the Project Manager or any other applicable team member.

5. Take phase reviews seriously

Phase reviews are designed to give Executive management a "snapshot" of the status of the product. Phase reviews are an excellent tool for confirming that processes are being followed and team deliverables are completed on time. If the Executive staff doesn't' take phase reviews seriously no one else will.

6. Make sure design reviews take place

Design reviews are necessary to confirm the product to be developed is realistic. Shortcutting the process at design will only increase the development process.

Summary of Deliverables for Phase – 2 – Planning

In Phase - 2 Team member deliverables include:
- Development designs and architects product
- Product Manager updates the Product Backlog
- Project Manager creates the team, Baseline Cost Document, and the Integrated Schedule

- Client Support, Development, Documentation, Marketing Communications, Product Marketing, Project Manager (if hardware), QA and Training each produce a plan for their department.

Phase 2 Summary by department

Client Support, Phase 2 – Planning
Receives business plan and design document, updates Product Backlog, creates client support plan and input for integrated schedule, provides Project Manager with cost information, attends meetings and Phase review.

Documentation, Phase 2 – Planning
Receives business plan and design document; creates marketing communications plan and input for integrated schedule, provides Project Manager with cost information, attends meetings and Phase review.

Development, Phase 2 – Planning
- Receives resources
- Designs and Architects product(s)
- Presents design at design review
- Presents design plan to team
- Works with team so associated departments can define their deliverables
- Inputs cost to Project Manager for Development Cost Baseline
- Creates the Development Plan
- Attends phase review

Marketing Communications, Phase 2 – Planning
- Receives Business Plan and Design Document,
- Creates Communications Plan
- Provides input for the Integrated Schedule,
- Provides Project Manager with cost information
- Attends meetings and Phase review.

Product Marketing, Phase 2 – Planning
- Takes over the Business Plan and updates it.
- Creates the Launch Plan
- Inputs schedule to Project Manager for integrated schedule
- Attends phase review

Project Manager Phase 2 – Planning
- Creates Project Team
- Initiates and runs weekly team meeting

- Creates and distributes Team Minutes
- Confirms Product Backlog is accurate and up-to-date
- Creates an integrated product schedule
- Creates Development Cost Baseline
- If hardware is being distributed creates the Roll Out Plan
- Presents integrated schedule and ROI to executive staff (Phase 2 Review)

Quality Assurance, Phase 2 – Planning
- Receives Business Plan and Design Document,
- Creates QA plan
- Provides input for integrated schedule,
- Provides Project Manager with cost information,
- Attends meetings and Phase review.

Training, Phase 2 – Planning
- Receives Business Plan and Design Document,
- Creates Training plan
- Provides input for integrated schedule,
- Provides Project Manager with cost information,
- Attends meetings and Phase review.

Documents Created in Phase 2

The following is detail on each new document created in this phase, in order of creation.

Design Document – This is a detailed architectural document created to explain the scope of the product along with the detail design specifications that will be implementing in the development phase of the product lifecycle.

Team Minutes – The team minutes are updated after each meeting. They record details on commitments, status, issues, requests, road blocks, and team decisions. They should be updated and published within 24 hours of a Project Team meeting.

Client Support Plan – The Client Support department develops a document that details what and how they will support the product, track bugs, provide services to clients and update clients with fixes.

Communications Plan – Marketing Communications creates a plan that identifies the PR, Advertising, articles, and promotions anticipated for this product.

Development Plan – The Development Manager identifies the number of developers needed to develop the product, skill sets and training is included in this plan.

Document Plan – Documentation creates a plan that outlines what documents will be developed, the scope of each document. Documentation needs to create a detailed outline that defines each of the chapters within the document and items this will be addressed within each chapter.

Launch Plan – Product Marketing creates a plan that identifies the material they will develop for Sales (presentations), collateral (brochures, white papers) Web updates, customer stories, presentations at conferences, and customer tours.

QA Plan – The QA manager creates a plan that identifies how they will QA the product. What the quality standards are, and how they will assure quality standards are met.

Roll Out Plan – created by the Project Manager if hardware purchased from 3rd party sources is part of the Client solution. This includes targets for receiving, staging, and installing the equipment along with targets of when vendors need to be chosen and estimated ship dates.

Training Plan – Training will meet with Client Support and Product Marketing to assure knowledge of the intended Client. They will create a plan that identifies type and scope of training programs for the product.

Development Cost Baseline –Each department provides the Project Manager with their expected costs. This information is used to updated the Baseline Cost Document created in Phase 1.

Integrated Schedule –This is a detailed schedule that can be developed using a computer based scheduling application that details all the deliverables, interdependencies, start and complete dates of each department highlighting all of the processes necessary to create this product.

Phase review presentation – given to executive staff.

Executive Sign Off – At the end of each phase review presentation, each member of the Executive staff reviews the phase sign off's, reflects on the information presented and decides if they agree to allow the product to proceed to the next stage of the product lifecycle. On the bottom of this document each executive signs his/her name and states if he/she approves or disapproves continuing to the next phase.

Phase Sign Off: – At the end of each phase, before the review presentation, each member of the Project Team reviews a document that contains information similar to that found in the Summary of Deliverables by Department section of this chapter. The Project Manager reviews this list in a team meeting and places the word complete or the date the deliverable will be completed by each team deliverable. The team then votes if they agree all deliverables have been met. Once the Project Team members are in agreement that all phase deliverables have been met, the team can present the product status at the phase review. The annotated Summary of Deliverables by Department sheet is attached to the Phase Sign-off document. The Phase Sign-off Document identifies the product, phase, and has a place for each member of the team and each executive to sign off if they agree the product meets the requirements of that phase and can move to the next phase.

Phase 3 – Scrum-Development

Phase 3 – Scrum-Development is when Agile Scrum is enacted and product increments are being created.

The Players in Phase 3

Members of the Project Team
- Client Support
- Development Manager
- Documentation Manager
- Marketing Communications
- Product Marketing
- Product Owner
- Project Manager
- QA Manager
- ScrumMaster
- Training Manger

Members of the Scrum Team
- Development Team: Developers, QA, Documentation
- Product Owner
- Scrum Master

Project Team Members:

Below is a sample list of people found on the Project Team for Phase 3, along with their team responsibility. Depending on the size and scope of your project your team members may vary.

Client Support – During Scrum-Development Support works with Product Marketing and QA to devise the Beta Plan, they attend Project Team and Sprint Review meetings.

Development Manager – Developers are part of the Development Team, but a manager is needed on the Project Team. The Development Manager works with Product Marketing and QA to devise the Beta Plan, they attend Project Team and Sprint Review meetings.

Documentation Manager – A documentation writer is part of the Development Team, but a manager is needed on the Project team. The Documentation Manager provides the Project Team with updates; they attend Project Team and Sprint Review meetings.

Marketing Communications – readies the Communication Plan, and they attend Project Team and Sprint Review meetings.

Product Marketing – Updates the Business Plan and creates the Announcement Plan. They also meet with the Development Manager and QA to create the Beta Plan. They attend Project Team and Sprint Review meetings.

Product Owner – is on both the Project Team and the Scrum Team. They are responsible for representing the Client and other stakeholders along with managing the Product Backlog. They attend Project Team and Sprint Review meetings. For internal products, the Product Owner is typically from a Client department. For external products, they may also be Product Marketing.

Project Manager – runs the Project Team meetings. If external software or hardware is to be purchased they work with the Development Manager to evaluate vendors. If the hardware needs to be sent to Clients they create the Roll-Out plan. They run the Project Team meetings and attend Sprint Review meetings.

QA Manager – QA is part of the Development Team. The QA Manager works with Product Marketing and the Development manager to create the Beta Plan. They attend Project Team and Sprint Review meetings.

ScrumMaster - is responsible for facilitating the Scrum process. They also attend the Project Team meeting. If there are multiple ScrumMaster's for one product, they either all attend the Project Meeting or one ScrumMaster is delegated with attending. Their goal is to facilitate increments and help train the organization on Scrum.

Training Manager – Training is responsible for creating all internal and external classes and online courses. They attend Project Team and Sprint Review meetings.

Scrum Team Members:

Development Team: A self-organizing cross-functional team of three to nine people that includes all the expertise necessary to deliver a potentially shippable increment each Sprint. The team should include QA and Documentation.

Product Owner: is responsible for maximizing return on investment by identifying product features, translating these into a prioritized list, deciding which features should be at the top of the list for the next Sprint, and continually re-prioritizing and refining the list. This person may also be the Product Manager.

ScrumMaster: helps the Development Team and the Project Team learn and apply Scrum to achieve business value. The ScrumMaster does whatever is in their power to help the Team.

Scrum Framework:

How The Scrum Process Works:

- Sprint
- Sprint Planning
- Daily Scrum
- The Sprint Burn Down Chart
- Product Backlog Refinement
- Sprint Review
- Sprint Retrospective

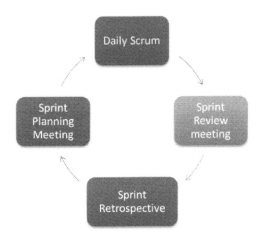

Figure 3-1 Sprint flow

Sprint - In the Scrum method of Agile development, work is confined to a regular, repeatable work cycle, known as a Sprint or increment. At the beginning of a project, the Development Team decides the length of each Sprint and continues this cycle for the life of the project. Scrum Sprints last from one to four weeks. When one Sprint ends the next Sprint starts. Each Sprint has four events: Sprint Planning, Daily Scrum, Sprint Review and Sprint Retrospective. Scrum also has three Artifacts, Product Backlog, Sprint Backlog and Increment.

Sprint Planning – Each Sprint starts with a planning meeting. The Development Team meets with the Product Owner and reviews the Product Backlog and discusses the high priority items. The Development Team and the Product Owner create a Sprint Goal and the Development Team chooses the top items from the Product Backlog to work on. These items are now called the Sprint Backlog. Next, the team agrees on the definition of Done for each item. The definition of Done incorporates what the Project Team has defined and now includes what the Development Team identifies as what it will take for each item in the Product Backlog to be shippable. This includes testing, QA, and Documentation.

When choosing the items the Development Team will complete this Sprint they must factor in holidays, vacation days, and overhead activities. Overhead activities typically include, technical debt, bug fixes, and support for existing products. After the items are chosen, the Product Owner leaves the room and the Development Team focuses on how they will execute this increment.

The integrated schedule exercise presented in the previous chapter is an excellent tool for the Development Team to deploy to come up with their Sprint plan. The ScrumMaster can facilitate the session. Each development activity including testing, QA and Documentation is written on a post-it and placed on a board. What becomes quickly obvious is how long it will take to create this increment and where interactions and hand-offs are needed. Team members can then negotiate to break activities into finer segments, so that they can more efficiently work with each other, and get their increment completed faster. At the end of the session, the team will have a mutually agreed upon working schedule for the Sprint. If the team realizes that they can't complete the quantity of work they have chosen, or that they have time for more work, this is the time for them to grab more items from the Product Backlog or return items to the Product Backlog.

Once the Sprint Planning meeting is concluded the Sprint Backlog is frozen. That is, no one can add or delete work to that Sprint. This is an extremely important rule. Nothing can hijack the productivity of a group faster and frustrate Developers more than changing tasks within a Sprint. Since Sprints are short in duration (one month or less), changing market conditions and management requests need to be factored into the Product Backlog, not the Sprint.

Daily Scrum - During the Sprint, at the same time every day, the Development Team holds a short Daily Scrum. This is a short meeting where each member of the Development Team provides three things: what they did the day before, what they will do today, and any roadblocks. Technical discussions are on hold until after all members of the team provide their three things. The ScrumMaster facilitates this meeting. The ScrumMaster takes the roadblocks as action items and uses what has been completed the day before to updated the Sprint Burn Down Chart.

Tip - Some Development Teams, especially if there are members located elsewhere, use their company's internal group communications platform to update each other on their three questions.

The Sprint Burn Down Chart – The Sprint Burn Down Chart is a graphical representation of work left to do versus time. Burn-downs charts are among the most common Sprint tracking mechanism.

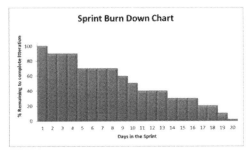

Figure 3-2 Sprint Burn Down Chart

The Sprint Burn chart displays the work remaining to do over time. The Team starts on day one with 100% of the Sprint Backlog to complete. For a one month Sprint, on day 20 they have completed all the work in the Sprint Backlog. For example, on days 2-4 of this chart, one Item is worked on and completed.

Product Backlog Refinement

During Scrum-Development it is necessary to groom or refine the Product Backlog. Grooming the Product Backlog becomes a Development Team responsibility. Less than ten percent of the Sprint should be spent on Product Backlog Refinement. Specifically, the Development Team performs detailed requirements analysis, splits large items into smaller ones, estimates the scope of new items, and re-estimates and clarifies the scope of existing items. Additionally, the team creates items that are functions, requirements, enhancements, and fixes. They add them to the Product Backlog.

Sprint Review – At the end of every Sprint is a Sprint Review. The entire Project Team and the Scrum Team are invited to the Sprint Review. The ScrumMaster facilitates this meeting. This meeting does not include PowerPoint presentations. It's when the Development Team showcases what they have been working on during the Sprint to the Project Team. The forum is casual, allowing members to provide feedback in order to allow the product to evolve.

Everyone at the review has the opportunity to concur if this increment meets the pre-defined definition of Done. If it does not meet the definition of Done, the increment is moved back into the Product Backlog to be re-prioritized and chosen to be worked on again. Next, the Product Owner leads a conversation about prioritization, stories, product, and client, to assure the Product Team and the Development Team are all headed in the same direction.

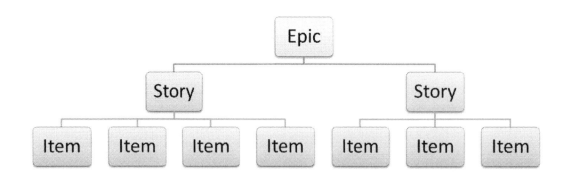

Figure 3-3 The Relationship between Item, Story, and Epic

The group now splits into two. The Development Team and the ScrumMaster move to the Sprint Retrospective; while the Project Team decides if the increment moves to Beta. Based on criteria developed in Phase 2, the Project Team decides if this increment should move to Beta or if it needs to wait and be combined with future increments to make a Story or an Epic, before moving to Beta. If the Project Team decides that the increment must wait for the rest of the Story or Epic before it is to be released, the completed increment is placed back in the Product Backlog with a notation "complete". When all the Items in a Story or Epic are Done, the Development Team chooses these Increments off the Product Backlog and integrates them so they are ready for Beta. This is called a Hardening Sprint.

Sprint Retrospective – Facilitated by the ScrumMaster, the Scrum Team discuss what's working and what's not working during the Sprint and agrees on changes to try. A popular method for assuring everyone has a voice in this meeting is for the ScrumMaster to hand out blank cards to everyone. Each member uses a card to write down, what's working, what's not working, and recommendations for more Sprint fluency. The ScrumMaster lists each card's comments on the board. The team discusses each comment and comes to an agreement on how better efficiency can be achieved.

After the Sprint Retrospective, the Team starts the next Sprint. Many teams plan the Sprint Review and Sprint Retrospective for a Friday and then schedule their Sprint Planning session for the following Monday morning.

Project Team Tasks

- Decide which Stories or Epics move to Beta
- Set severity levels for the Beta and Released product and identify escalation paths.
- Identify Beta Clients and the Beta Plan
- Review the Product Release Plan
- Review the Announcement Plan
- Review changes in the Product Backlog and provides feedback to the Product Owner
- Attend Sprint Review meetings
- If applicable hardware is chosen and ordered

During Scrum-Development, the other members of the Project Team are planning for Beta and Release by staying current with the product.

Moving Increments to Beta

The Project Team decides which completed increments, Stories or Epics will be moved to Beta. Typically this is when they enact the plan they created in Phase 2.

During Product Backlog Refinement, the Development Team breaks a Story into Tasks that can be completed in one Sprint cycle. Even though an increment meets the definition of Done, it doesn't mean it is appropriate to move the increment to Beta. Typically teams will want to only move completed Stories or Epics to Beta. During Development the Project Team needs to keep track of Stories as they get broken down to tasks so that when all the tasks that make up a Story are completed they can be moved to Beta.

Setting severity levels – Your Development organization should already have a grading system whereby when Client Support is notified there is a bug, Client Support can identify the severity of that bug. For instance, the severity rating can run from 1 to 5, one being the worst. A severity 1 bug would notify the organization that the bug crashes the system while a severity 5 bug could mean that punctuation in a message is incorrect.

Management from QA, Client Support, and Development need to review the severity rating system and make sure they agree on what types of errors fall into which categories. An escalation path also needs to be identified. This escalation path should include organizations and expected time for resolution. Even if your organization has this grading system and escalation path in place, it is wise to review it and confirm that it meets the needs of the team.

Product Backlog is reviewed and updated – The Product Owner and the Development Team each update the Product Backlog. The Product Owner is adding in new Stories and re-prioritizing Stories and Tasks, while the Development Team is turning Stories into Tasks and adding in additional development tasks. The Project Team should be notified of changes to the Product Backlog after Product Backlog Refinement so they can better plan for their deliverables.

The Beta Plan

The Beta Plan is a document that outlines how the beta will be conducted, who will receive the beta product and how the Project Team will manage the Beta.
- The Project Team decides what type of Beta the Story will need.
- Beta's can be Public – open to everyone, Closed – open to a select group of people or Hybrid – starts out closed and open up to everyone.
- The QA Manager drafts a document outlining the requirements for the Beta Clients.
- The QA Manager work with Product Marketing to draft a questionnaire for Beta sites to answer that assures they meet the Project Team's needs

It's True: Beta is when a select group of clients uses the Story.

No increment should ever move directly to General Available. No matter how thorough the Development Team is in meeting the definition of Done, problems including bugs, latency and scalability issues can still exist. To minimize risk, every Story should go through a period of time when it is released to a controlled group.

The Project Team will decide the appropriate Beta period for the Story. This decision will be based on the type of Story being developed and the Client's sophistication and needs. A Beta period can run a week, or it can run for months. The issue for the Project Team is assuring the features, latency, and scalability has been properly exercised.

Betas are either public, closed, or a hybrid of both. A Closed Beta is when the organization gives the Story to a select group of Clients for testing. A Public Beta is when the organization opens the Beta up to a select group of the general public. For a web app, Clients may opt-in to access a Beta Story, or the Product Team might decide that a randomly chosen percentage of Clients will have access to the new Story. A Hybrid Beta is a Closed Beta that turns into an Open Beta.

For example, if your product is an App intended for employees, before distributing the App to every employee, you should choose a small target group of employees who will assure the App works as expected. If you are distributing the App to the general marketplace, identify a group of clients who will receive it first and are prepared to exercise the features, or limit the number of people that can access this App.

A Hybrid Beta starts out as a Closed Beta and at a predetermined time is moved to a Public Beta. For example, an organization with a three-month Beta starts with a closed beta for two months. If the feedback on the Story is good, then the Project Team can open the Beta up to a portion of the general population for one month. Even though the Public Beta sounds like general availability, by calling it Beta the Project Team can limit access while closely monitor what's going on. Meanwhile, the Development Team is still identified as resources for the Story.

Pro's and con's to a public beta: On the pro side, potential Clients can take the Story for a spin and figure out if they like using it. On the con side, Beta stories may not be stable and may not be feature rich. Providing buggy features that have not been fully tested to the masses may result in bad press and support headaches. Public Betas tend to reflect a company's philosophical outlook. Some organizations like to continually share new services with their clients. Their philosophy is, "look at the cool stuff we are creating, we're running rings around the competition." With their clients, their position is, "stay with us and be the first kid on the block to get this kind of functionality." Another benefit to a Public Beta is, it's typically difficult to find Clients willing to test-drive beta applications. Running a public beta provides a potentially large group of people to test your Story.

If your organization decides to conduct a Public Beta, the Product Team is responsible for aligning your Beta philosophically with your organization. Identify if a Public Beta is right for your Story. If a Story needs a lot of handholding, support, or if you're Clients are temperamental or impatient, you might be better off deploying a Closed Beta.

Regardless if the beta is closed or public, during Scrum-Development, the Development Manager, Product Marketing, and the QA Manager need to meet to develop the Beta Plan and create the Client Beta questionnaire. For Public Beta's, it's helpful to provide a simple survey. It has been found that giving away a T-shirt drastically increases the number of people who take a survey.

An example of a Beta specification for a Closed Beta is:

- It will be necessary to Beta this Story with a minimum of ten Clients to a maximum of 100 Clients over a four-week Beta cycle.
- Customer Support is the front line of support, they use existing processes to log in any questions.
- Quality Assurance is responsible for managing the Beta sites and is responsible for checking to see how often the beta clients use the story.
- QA is tasked with reporting back to the team on any comments or issues.

The Beta plan consists of a list of action items that will ensure a successful Beta. Specifically, it identifies who in the organization is responsible for the action items and assigns a begin and end data to assure that the Beta will begin and end on time. Here is an example.

Task	Department
Identify potential Beta clients, create a public beta site	Product Marketing (PM)
Minimum configuration and features tested	QA/Development
Draft Beta questionnaire	PM and QA
Clients information	QA
Prepare checklist of technologies to be tested	QA
Bring Beta site information to Project Team	PM
Prepare Beta use contract	Legal
Monitor Beta progress	Client Support or QA

3-3 Beta Plan

Identifying Beta Clients

- Product Marketing works with Sales, Client Support, and the Client community to identify potential Beta Sites
- For a Closed Beta, these sites are interviewed to assure that they meet the Project Team's needs
- For an Open Beta, the Project Team qualifies beta clients via a set of requirements

Tip: Sign up twice as many Beta Clients as needed. Many times Clients get busy and don't have a chance to exercise a product.

Identifying Beta sites – If the Project Team decides on a Closed Beta, Product Marketing is tasked with finding Beta sites and QA certifies the sites as Beta Clients. Product Marketing may work with Sales to identify Clients who would be good prospective Beta sites. Finding good Beta sites is probably one of the most difficult tasks of the Beta program. Many Clients do not have the facilities or time to test a Story properly. Most Clients who are interested in testing a Story most likely need the Story in full production mode since it solves a problem they are experiencing. This can cause potential problems since the team is still working out bugs and many Clients have a low tolerance for errors. It is very important to impress upon clients that this Story is Beta quality, which means it has been tested internally but still has a high probability of having bugs.

If this Story is for an external Client application and the organization decides to go with a Public Beta, finding Beta Clients will be easier. Your support infrastructure for the Beta Clients should be identified and created during this phase. At the least, you will need to put a legal disclaimer on your website that Clients will need to click through before accessing the Story. If appropriate, ask Beta Clients to provide their e-mail or whatever you use to communicate with them. This way they can be notified when a new release is made available. Other services that are beneficial to include with a Public Beta are a bulletin board identifying known bugs and dates when the bug fixes will be available, a bulletin board where Beta Clients can ask questions and inform you about bugs they are experiencing, and a short video that shows clients how to use this Story.

It's best to sign up twice as many Beta Clients as the Project Team specified since there's a high probability that up to 50% of Beta Clients will not be able to test the Story during the allotted time. It's wise to remember that Beta sites are doing the Product Team a favor. Treat them accordingly. If a good relationship developed with a Beta Client, the next time a Story enters Beta, the Client usually is willing to be a participant.

Evaluating Vendors

If this project includes the procurement and distribution of new equipment, the Project Manager and Development Manager are tasked with reviewing different vendor's solutions. A Roll Out Plan identifying how to proceed with identifying new equipment should have been created in Phase 2. The Project Manager and Development Manager bring complimentary skills and perspective of what makes a good solution to the table. There are a few simple guidelines for successfully choosing a vendor.

Make a List – Make sure you have a complete list of vendors that provide the solution you are looking for.

Keep an Open Mind – A vendor's sales person may have been working with your Development Team for a long time. They may have spearheaded the product. The teams' responsibility is to the organization and the product, not a vendor. Keep an open mind, review multiple solutions, you may be surprised what you find. Salespeople have a way of disappearing after they sell a solution. Your job is to assure the organization receives the best solution.

Use your Design Document – Vendors will provide you with their list of features. This is your product. You need to be assured that the solution meets all your "A" level requirements.

Check references – Talk to at least three clients who have installed and used the solution. If the vendor doesn't have three referenceable clients – run! Make sure the referenceable clients are using the solution in a production environment. The vendor should be able to provide you with a list of clients that you call and talk to. For large products, the Project Manager should talk to the person who has a similar job at the reference organization. Product Marketing can talk to their pier at the reference organization, while the Development Manager talks to their pier at the reference organization. For smaller products, you will only need to talk to one person at the reference organization. The goal of these conversations is to assure the solution works as promised and the organization supports clients after they purchase the product.

The Release Plan

- The release plan identifies what is needed to get the product out the door.
- Regardless of the complexity of the product, a key person needs to be identified who is responsible for the release of the product.
- If this product includes hardware (e.g. supplying employees with a Smartphone or Tablet) a key member needs to be identified to be responsible for assuring equipment order is received, configured, and sent on to the appropriate person.

The Project Manager is responsible for developing the Release Plan. This plan might be as simple as a one-page document stating the link to the new application will be available for the webmaster to post on a specific day, or the new features will be integrated with the existing product and available for access on a specific day.

For complex products that include new hardware and software, a key operations person needs to be identified who is responsible for the physical release of the product. This person needs to understand what is being received and by whom, who is responsible for putting the pieces together, and who receives the completed solution e.g. what software will be installed on employees phones. Possible elements in a Release Plan are, identifying people responsible for staging, training, dates for training, and a staging location. Copies of the staging plan along with itemized staging tasks should be created and disseminated before staging takes place.

A product that works wonderfully in the lab but is not staged properly will be a disaster. Clients do not react well to receiving bits and pieces of a solution. From the client's point of view, every solution needs to be plug-and-play. Spend the time up front detailing the release plan.

The Announcement Plan

Creating a plan: Marketing Communications and Product Marketing create an Announcement Plan that identifies which Stories or Epics will be marketed. Part of the Announcement Plan includes creating a budget and obtaining budget approval.

For each marketed Story or Epic, the plan should detail, what specifically will be done including an official announcement, contacting press, advertising, social media, in product notifications, and e-mail notifications.

For worldwide products, translations need to be made for each target country's language and culture. If the announcement is to be simultaneously occurring, worldwide schedules need to be built that allow time for localization. An effective American campaign does not always play in Europe. The plan details if materials developed will be deployed around the world or if new materials will be developed for each market. Budgets, politics, and client's demographics play into this decision.

Product Marketing and Communication's Role – Product Marketing should be intimately familiar with the needs of the Clients and the product. Marketing Communications is intimately familiar with getting the word out internally and for external communications, they are familiar with the press, industry analysts, and advertising channels. Marketing Communications has a tight pulse on the current themes the press is writing about and can recommend the best way to present the product to the clients verbally and visually. Marketing Communications is responsible for managing the announcement process and the message since deliverables may come from many people, both internal and external to the organization.

Marketing Communications and Product Marketing are tasked with deciding how, where and when it is best to announce this product. If the team decided on a public beta, this launch may be actualized at the beginning of beta. If this is a closed beta the launch will be actualized at the end of beta. Depending on the product and the visibility of the organization, it may be wise to announce the product in conjunction with an industry event. Whereas some products obtain better visibility when released during slack news periods. Considerations that affect the announcement date may be competitive launches and newsworthy subjects that can gain better visibility for the product. For example, a new sales tool can be announced at the organization's yearly sales meeting, or a security application can be announced in coordination with a Human Resources security program.

For external announcements, organizations should be careful not to introduce a product too soon. A competitor's announcement may drive an organization to feel they need to introduce a product early. This approach can backfire. Press and analysts take into account release dates and reference-able Beta sites. When release dates are far out and Beta sites cannot be spoken to, the press and analysts notice and highlight the immaturity of the announcement. Organizations should choose their announcement date based on what would gain them the most positive press. It is unwise to lose the momentum of an announcement by being viewed as a "me too" announcement.

A better strategy is to give the competitor time to deliver. If the competitor announces too early, their product release date can slip or their product's quality may be poor. If your organization announces later, but delivers and executes as planned, you will have an advantage.

Some organizations entice the press by overhanging the market. Overhanging the market is a strategy used to get the press and bloggers to speculate about a soon to be released product by trickling out information. For instance, vendor A is coming out with a new smartphone next quarter. They trickle out very little information, just enough to get in the news. Finally, they announce the phone at a big event with lots of giant pictures of the phone. Competitor B is also planning on releasing a new phone. Competitor B's phone is still in development. If Vendor A's phone is late, or it's quality is poor, competitor B can use A's announcement and shortcomings as a competitive advantage.

The Announcement Plan: The areas to be considered when creating a Product Announcement Plan are: message development, contacting journalists and bloggers, announcement date, product release deliverables, and advertising.

Message Development – Product Marketing works closely with Marketing Communications to develop a complete message. It is the responsibility of the corporate officers to provide corporate direction and the corporate message. It is the responsibility of Marketing Communications to take this message and direction and articulate it. Product Marketing is responsible for providing product positioning and demographic information so that Marketing Communications can create a positioning statement that will properly target the clients. The product and corporate message are the fundamental ideas behind a product release. It is necessary for the corporate message to incorporate the product message and for each to be in concert with the other.

The organization's market position needs to be taken into account when releasing a new product. Before a product release, any updates to corporate positioning should be made. Corporate positioning explains who the organization is and how they view themselves. The corporate presentation defines the organization's target market and the position they have within the market. Product positioning explains who the market is, what need this product fulfills, why this need is important, why this product fills that need.

When creating an advertising campaign, Copy Writers are used to properly articulate the message, while artists create an appropriate design for the product. A design is developed to match the Clients with the product. For example, the graphics on a can of motor oil has a very different design than the graphics found on a jar of bath oil. Would bath oil sell if it were packaged with an industrial design, would motor oil sell if it was designed with romantic script? The design considers all elements including branding, typeface, graphics and display format.

Contacting Journalists – For newsworthy releases, a list of analysts that influence the financial markets, press, and influential bloggers need to be identified. Marketing Communications are responsible for identifying the correct analyst, checking if any upcoming reports are applicable, reviewing the reports for impact, and developing a strategy of how best to update the analysts. The client's demographic information is used to identify which media should be pitched to. Marketing Communications works with the organization's Public Relations (PR) firm to identify the themes that need to be developed for pitching the Stories or Epics.

Communication should identify an appropriate position for each publication and then find the writer responsible for covering this market. Marketing Communications needs to identify if certain analysts and press will receive the information early or if they will receive the information during a specified press tour.

Product Announcement – An appropriate date needs to be chosen to announce the increment, story, or epic. Before the announcement date, "friendly" bloggers and press need to be met with so they have time to review the release and write their story. For large international releases an East Coast, West Coast, European and Asian press tour needs to be defined and appointments scheduled. A good PR firm is instrumental in assisting in this process. The PR firm will help identify the press and analysts, and identify how upcoming Stories or Epics will fit into planned editorial themes. They'll set the schedule for the press tour and review the deliverables to make sure they are clear and targeted.

Product Release Deliverables – Depending on the type of release, announcement deliverables need to be developed. For an internal release, it might be as simple as an e-mail to all employees. It might expand to a banner announcing the new product displayed in the entranceway to the organizations building or cafeteria, or a web page banner on the organization's intranet site linking to the new application. If the product is for external clients or the general marketplace deliverables may also include e-mails, web banners, videos, tweets, blogs, social media or mailers.

Advertising – If appropriate, advertising needs to be created. The client's demographic information is used to determine the most effective advertising campaign. Magazine ads, online advertising, website banners, direct mail, video's, Social Media and Twitter messages need to be laid out, scripted, designed and coordinated.

The Phase 3 – Development – Presentation

The cornerstone of Scrum-Development is consistently releasing increments. Since Scrum-Development, Beta, and General Availability are a continual cycle, there is no individual Scrum-Development, Beta, and General Availability presentation to executive management. Instead, organizations that implement Scrum needs to set a regular schedule when management reviews each product. This can be quarterly, half yearly or yearly. This presentation encompasses Scrum Development, Beta, and Release. In this meeting the Project Manager provides the following:

- Updated Business Plan – changes from the original and the last presentation
- Client Needs
- Product environment
- Product Backlog
- Increment history
- Increments done
- Increments approved for client access
- Beta overview
- Release overview

- Marketing Communications Plan

Sample Phase 3 Presentation Outline:

Page 1: Cover Page. This document should be for controlled distribution, List the names of all the people attending and receiving the review handout. The cover page should have the product name, the phase, and the date.

Page 2: Agenda. List major issues that will be presenting, the time allotted. Agenda items for a Phase 3 review may be: introduction, Story release status, team overview, issues and risks

Page 3: Development Phase 3: Review the items that have been developed since the last presentation
- Actual feature / functionality developed
- Any changes from Design to Development is highlighted
- Code review is performed
- QA verification testing complete
- Documentation draft documents presented to the team
- Beta test plan defined

Page 4: Last phase review action item completion status, list action, and current status. (After the last review executive staff may have requested action items take place. List those action items along with the status for each item.)

Page 5: Contract Summary: If contracts were signed for hardware, software, support services, or networking equipment the estimated vs actual costs should be listed along with any pertinent legal obligations.

Page 6: Integrated schedule: List the characteristics of Done, requirements for an increment to be released to clients, Beta plan, and release plan.

Page 7: Updated Development costs: List the following items by employee weeks and capital costs for the current phase and the previous phase. Marketing, Development, and Client Support.

Page 8: Team Members. List all the members of the Project Team and the functional areas they represent.

Page 9: Team Status cover sheet. The following sheets highlight the team deliverables that have been created by team members.

Page 10: Issues and Risks for this phase: List issue, owner, risk, impact, and status.

Page 11: Executive Session: Executive sign off, Executives note any action items for the team and agree to let the program move to the next phase.

Recommendations for Management and Team Members

Management Recommendations:
- Manage don't dictate – If the product runs into problems don't dictate a solution, let the team come back with solutions and choose the approach that meets the organization's needs.
- Take phase reviews seriously – Phase reviews are designed to give executive management a "snapshot" onto the status of the product. They are an excellent tool for confirming processes are being followed and team deliverables are completed on time. If the executive staff doesn't' take phase reviews seriously no one else will.
- Recommendations for successfully managing Scrum Teams – Managing a Scrum Team is different than a traditional Development Team. Specifically because of the short timebox nature of Sprints and the philosophy that Development Teams are self-organizing. For Scrum Teams to work at peak efficiency, the following rules need to be followed.
- Don't change the Sprint Backlog within a Sprint – management is use to asking a developer to add a feature or make changes on the fly. Since Sprints are short and focused, they should never be changed. Management influences development by working with the Product Owner to add or change a Story and to change priorities in the Product Backlog.
- Don't ask "when will this be done?" – Development within a Sprint is calibrated for that Sprint. Within a Sprint the Development Team decides the priority of creating features. The answer for when this will be done is, "At the end of the Sprint." Don't waist Developer cycles, let them focus on their work.
- Don't make a Development Manager or any other Line Manager the Sprint Master – Development Teams are self-organizing. A senior manager has undue influence and will start overriding team decisions. Within a Sprint let the team focus on their deliverables.
- Don't just use Scrum expressions, support Scrum behaviors.

Project Team Recommendations:
- Don't blame, find solutions

Summary of Deliverables by Department in Phase 3

In Phase - 3 Project Team members' deliverables include:
- Developing increments

- Agreeing if an increment is Done based on the pre-determined definition of Done.
- Moving an Increment either to Beta or back to the Product Backlog as it waits either for integration or the remaining increments in its Story to be completed.
- Product Marketing and the QA Manger develops the Beta Plan and identifies Beta Clients.
- If there is Hardware to be purchased the Project Manager and the Development Manager will review vendor solutions.
- The Project Manager creates a Release Plan
- Product Marketing and Marketing Communications create the Announcement Plan.

Client Support – Phase 3
- Works with Client Support and Product Marketing to create Beta Plan
- Receives and reviews product Documentation
- Attends all Project Team and Sprint Review meetings

Development Manager – Phase 3
- Works with Client Support and Product Marketing to create Beta Plan
- Works with the Project Manager to review vendor solutions (if hardware needs to be purchased.)
- Attends all Project Team and Sprint Review meetings

Marketing Communications – Phase 3
- Readies the Communication Plan
- Attends all Project Team and Sprint Review meetings

Product Marketing Phase 3 – Development
- Works with the Development Manager and Client Support, and QA to create the Beta Plan
- Creates the Announcement Plan
- Attends all Project Team and Sprint Review meetings

Project Manager Phase 3 – Development
- Confirms Beta plan is created
- Works with the Development Manager to execute the Roll Out Plan, if necessary.
- Creates Release Plan
- Facilitates information flows within Project Team
- Works with Development Team to identify vendors and negotiate contracts
- Runs all Project Team meetings and attends Sprint Review meetings

QA Manager Phase 3 – Development

- Assures QA and Documentation meet definition of Done
- Works with Client Support to create Escalation Procedures
- Meets with Product Marketing, Client Support, and Development Manger to define Beta Plan
- Attends all Project Team and Sprint Review meetings

Scrum Team – Phase 3
- Develops increments
- Follows Scrum framework

Training Manger
- Creates training based on Story release cycle
- Attends all Project Team and Sprint Review meetings

Documents Created in Phase 3 Development

Phase 3 is when the product is executed the following documents are created:
- The Beta Plan
- The Beta Questionnaire
- Escalation Procedures
- The Release Plan
- The Announcement Plan

Beta Plan –The Beta plan is a document developed by Product Marketing and QA. The purpose of a Beta plan is to define the roles and responsibilities the people participating in the Beta process. The Beta plan details qualifications to become a Beta site along with technologies and procedures the Beta sites will be testing.

Beta Questionnaire –The survey questions given to clients' needs to be created.

Escalation Procedures – The QA Manger works with Client Support and the Development Manager to develop a detailed plan outlining escalation procedures and definitions for bug severity.

The Release Plan – Product Marketing produces a plan that identifies the procedure of moving stories and Epics to Beta and Release

The Announcement Plan – Marketing Communications works with Product Marketing to identify which Stories or Epics will be announced and the level of announcement for each Story.

Phase 4 – Beta

During Phase 4 – Beta, Client Support, and QA take the lead to resolve Beta Client needs.
- Beta is performed to assure the product meets organization standards for quality.
- Product Marketing is focused on actualizing the Announcement Plan
- Marketing Communications is focused on actualizing the Communication Plan
- A Beta Committee is formed with Client Support, QA, and the Development Manager
- The Project Manager confirms that the Release Plan is completed and ready for execution.

Beta takes place after the Story or Epic meets the definition of Done and the Project Team votes that it should be released to customers. If the Project Team decided to create a closed Beta, the Story is made available to a select group of Clients. These Clients have agreed to use the Story and confirm that the Story meets their needs and works in their environment.

If it has been decided that the Story will be tested in a Public Beta the product is made available to a wider group of people. If the Clients are outside the organization and this is a Public Beta, the Story may be officially launched during this phase.

The Beta Committee – A Beta review committee should be established by QA at the start of the Beta period. This committee consists of QA, Development and a Client Support. QA runs the meeting. The purpose of this committee is to foster communication between these three organizations and provide each area with a forum to review the Beta site activities. The committee needs to be aware of which Clients have the product, their use, and any problems that arise. The goal of this committee ensures that issues, bugs, and client confusion are funneled to the right people and properly addressed in an appropriate amount of time.

During Beta, Clients with questions call into Client Support where their call is logged. Quality Assurance then takes the lead by testing to see if the issue is a bug or a breakdown in understanding. QA brings all questions to the Beta Committee so that issues are visible and the committee can identify where the issue falls so they can facilitate resolution. Meanwhile, Product Marketing and Marketing Communications focus on actualizing the Communications Plan and the Announcement Plan. While the Project Manager assures the Release Plan is in place and ready.

Hybrid Beta – For a Hybrid Beta, the Project Team sets up procedures for a Closed Beta and a Public Beta. The Project Team will identify a series of triggers – behaviors that will tell the team that the Story is mature enough to be moved from a Closed Beta to a Public Beta. Triggers might be as simple as, the Story moves from closed to open if there is confirmed usage and no high severity problems.

Phase 4 – Beta Players

- Client Support
- Development Manager
- Marketing Communications
- Product Manager
- Project Manager
- Quality Assurance Manager
- Training Manager

Client Support –All Beta client questions should go through Client Support. Client Support logs the question and works with QA to identify if this is a Bug or an area that needs more training. As Stories or Epics are released to Beta, Client Support needs to be trained on supporting these features.

Development Manager –Development is a key organization in Beta since they need to fix bugs on a timely basis. Fixing bugs should always be a high priority Item in the Sprint Backlog. Based on experience, the Development Team needs to set aside enough time to manage bugs.

Documentation Manager – Documentation for the Story is made available to Client Support and Customers. Client Support provides Documentation with their own and Client feedback so that adjustments can be made.

Marketing Communications – begins to execute the Communications Plan.

Product Marketing – Composes release materials for the Story, works with Marketing Communications where necessary to support the Communications Plan, and works with Sales to make sure they are trained and ready to sell the Story.

Product Owner – Updates the Product Backlog if they identify new Stories.

Project Manager – Assures the Beta sites have access to the Story, and those customers who call into Client Support with issues are receiving timely answers.

QA Manager – Client Support logs Client question while QA is responsible for identifying if this is a Bug or an area that needs more training. QA brings all Client questions back to the Development Team so they can get a better understating of how the Client is using the Story. When QA identifies a bug, they notify their fellow members of the Development Team to fix it. QA needs to estimate the time they spend on Beta support and make sure it's accounted for in the Sprint Backlog.

ScrumMaster – Keeps apprised of the Beta sites and facilitates communication between the Project Team and the Development team.

Training Manager – Initial training is conducted. Feedback is received and changes, if necessary, is made.

Monitored Release Product

For complex products, the team might feel the beta period did not provide the extensive testing needed. Due to business pressures, the Story needs to be released.
- A monitored release allows Stories or Epics with limited testing to be released.
- To expedite problems the beta team stays in place during a monitored release.
- Monitored release provides the team with higher levels of insight into clients receiving monitored release products.

Definition of a Monitored Release – The Monitored Release status gives a Project Team the ability to, monitor which clients receive a Story, visibility into problems; the authority, responsibility, and the budget to assure the Story works as specified. The monitored status ensures QA and Development are still allocating time to fix bugs and the Project Team is working with Client Support to assure there are no outstanding problems.

Monitored releases are not needed if you have a Hybrid Beta since you have an opportunity for a wider audience to test your product before it is released. Sometimes Hybrid Betas are not feasible and the Project Team feels the Beta period did not provide the extensive testing needed. Stories cannot stay in beta forever; teams need to release Stories.

When the Project Team feels the Story is stable but wants to maintain close control over the released Story they create a Monitored Release. Sophisticated products, those with interdependencies, accessing multiple systems that require verification, or require extensive training may be a good candidate for a Monitored Release.

If the solution includes hardware, the Project Manager uses Beta to test their procurement and roll out processes defined in the Roll Out Plan.

During Beta, the Project Team needs to decide how the Story should be released. Should the Story be sent out freely? Does the Project Team need to monitor the release? A Monitored Release is not related to quality but to scope. Some Stories are so all encompassing no Beta site will ever be able to properly test the Story in all situations. A Monitored Release provides the Project Team with a step between Beta and General Availability. That is the Project Team still receives access into who is receiving the Story, how many people are using the Story, and the types of calls Support is receiving; while also keeping the Beta Committee in place. This way, if a problem arises; the Project Team knows the level of exposure.

Ending Beta

The following deliverables need to be complete for Beta to end:
- Documentation and Training are completed
- Marketing Communications is ready to announce
- There are no known severity 1 or 2 bugs
- The Release Plan is in place and ready
- The Project Manager updates the financial and releases information.
- At the end of the Beta timebox, when all the deliverables are completed, the Project Team votes to move the Story from Beta to Availability.

Recommendations for Management and the Team

Management Recommendations
- Don't release bad code –fixing a bug in the field is ten times more expensive than fixing a bug before the product is released. Poor quality products do not help the Clients.

Recommendations for the team
- Hold a beta team debriefing session. This is similar to a Sprint Retrospective. To get candid comments the Product Manager can use a similar exercise to the one the ScrumMaster uses. Or, by going online and typing in "Sprint Retrospective games", you can find a number of exercises that facilitate communication.

Team Member's Roles

Each team member was responsible for executing a number of tasks.
- Client Support Manager
- Development Manager
- Documentation Manager
- Marketing Communications
- Product Marketing
- Project Manager
- Quality Assurance Manager
- Training Manger

Client Support – During Beta they take Client calls; is a member of the Client Beta Committee along with QA and Development, and are trained on the Story.

Development Team – Fixes bugs and receives feedback on Client usage.

Documentation – Provides QA, Client Support and Beta customers with draft docs. Continues to update docs throughout Beta.

Marketing Communications – *For an internal announcement* – writes copy for an organization-wide notification. Places appropriate notifications announcing the new Story within internal web site. Receives approval for banners to be hung in the cafeterias or office entrances. *For an external announcement* – Completes press kit and product collateral, interviews Beta Clients and completes case studies if appropriate, stages press tour, places ads, and define how ads will be monitored for effectiveness, create communications message for bloggers and social media.

Product Marketing – assures that collateral is ready, supports Marketing Communications, provides Press and analysts with information.

Project Manager – Confirms that Product Marketing is executing the Announcement Plan while Marketing Communications is executing the Communications Plan, along with confirming that the Release Plan is complete and ready to be executed, confirms any Client equipment has been ordered and will be received on time; If appropriate, tests the Roll Out Plan by setting up staging areas and confirms people are available, trained and ready to send and receive equipment; along with assuring any software contracts have been signed.

QA – Takes the lead on the Beta Committee, manages the Beta Clients after Client Support logs any calls. Continues to test the Story, reproduces Beta bugs, confirms that bugs are fixed.

Training – Completes training courses and updates them based on Client feedback.

Phase 5 – General Availability

General availability is when the Story or Epic is released and is in full production by the clients. Maintaining the product includes:
- Client Support
- Training
- Scheduled upgrades
- Development Team–fixes bugs

The people involved in the day-to-day sustaining activities are:
- Client Support
- Training

General availability is when the Story is in use by the Clients. If the proper due diligence was performed when setting the definition of Done and in Beta, the product should be relatively bug-free. Sustaining costs will be incurred for the Story, this may include the cost of Client Support, training, scheduled software or hardware upgrades, and the people within the organization responsible for maintaining the infrastructure.

On a yearly basis, Executive Management reviews the product to assure fit and reasonable maintenance costs. If the organization has planned a new Story or Product that will obsolete the current product, a general availability review should still be performed.

It is valuable to take the time to review the acceptance of the product and compare this to predictions. Typically organizations are so focused on releasing the next version they don't take the time to review the acceptance of the current product. Yearly reviews are an invaluable tool in understanding how close earlier estimates are to reality. The Phase 5 review gives the organization valuable information that can be used to fine tune and benchmark the process.

The Player's in Phase 5 are:

- Client Support
- Development Manager
- Marketing Communications
- Product Manager
- Product Owner
- Project Management

- Quality Assurance Manager
- Training Manager

Client Support – Works with the client, logs all calls, escalates bugs to Development.

Development Manager – Tracks the time developers spend on sustaining (bug) issues. Works with Client Support to decide if a Client complaint is a bug, a new feature, or a limitation in documentation or training. New feature requests are sent to the Product Owner.

Marketing Communications – Executes the Communications plan.

Product Marketing – Works with Sales to provide marketing programs.

Product Owner – Adds feature requests from Sales and Client support to the Product Backlog.

Project Manager – Comes back to the team to prepare the 360 review.

Product Release

Release is the small amount of time between when Beta ends and the Story becomes generally available. During Release, all the last minute details come together. The Project Team is responsible for assuring the Release goes smoothly.
- Client Support confirms they are prepared to take questions
- Documentation assures that all the documentation is final and ready
- Training confirms that their classes are available to Clients.
- The Project Manager actualizes the Release Plan.
- Product Marketing assures that Sales is trained and ready.

Release is a chaotic time. It has been compared to having the family over for Thanksgiving Day dinner. No matter how organized the cook, they always spend Thanksgiving Day in the kitchen cooking.

At release, all the last minute details come together and the team members are responsible for assuring everything goes smoothly.

If applicable, Marketing Communications executes the Communications Plan by releasing the press release, has journalists and bloggers lined up to talk about the product, has put together a social media plan and has created the advertising material.

If the Story was announced during a Public Beta, documents might need to be updated and a press release announcing general availability can be sent out.
- Client Support confirms their organization is trained and ready to support Clients.
- The Training department confirms that their classes are finalized and available to Clients.

- Product Marketing confirms that Sales is trained, has pricing and product information.
- The Project Manager actualizes the Release Plan and updates the Product's financials.
- The Project Team meets to review assignments and confirm that all deliverables are complete.

Tip: A good policy is to follow the release meeting with a party and awards. The Scrum Team should be included.

During General Availability:

The product is in use as new Stories are added. Yearly the product should be reviewed for effectiveness.
- Review estimated versus actual costs to maintain the product
- Review Client Support issues
- Review Training costs
- Identify client penetration, and decide if an update or follow on product is needed.

A product review should take place after the product has been released and has been available for the past year. Don't overlook yearly phase reviews on released products. It is very important for an organization to track its accuracy for predicting costs and meeting organizational goals. A general availability phase review provides a yearly forum for executives to view product success.

The Yearly Review meeting is not a sales or territory review, sales figures should not be discussed. The Yearly Review's purpose is to: review estimated versus actual costs to maintain the product, review Client Support issues, training costs, the program's effectiveness, identify client penetration, and decide if an update or follow on product is needed. The review highlights areas that the organization needs to address. For instance, if bugs are higher than anticipated Development might be asked to review why there are more problems than anticipated. This information can be used to intervene and add sustaining budget to a released product, better predict the sustaining costs of future products or result in different test procedures run during QA.

Marketing Communications is usually busy during Availability. Ongoing advertising, blogging, and social media are very important to maintain the visibility of a product.

Maintaining a product once it is released
- Daily maintenance needs to take place
- Bugs need to be tracked and fixed

- Training and support need to be available

It's True: The Project Team decides if a bug is a fix for something broken or a new feature.

An example of deciding what is a bug or a new feature: A Client calls Client Support because they don't like the way a fill-in-screen works. The fill-in-screen works as defined in the Story. After Development and QA presents that the fill-in-screen works as designed, the Product Owner may decide to change the design. They can add this new Story to the Product Backlog.

Fixing Bugs – Fixing a released Story is referred to as sustaining Development. Some organizations make the developers who created the Story, responsible for fixing problems once the Story is available. There are pros and cons to using the same people for new development and sustaining development. On the pro side, the creators will fix what they designed or developed. This may be beneficial since they are familiar with what they developed. It also can drive them to design products that are easier to fix since they know they will be responsible later.

On the con side, having programmers working on a new Story while being responsible for fixing sustaining problems, can cause Sprints to be incomplete. A hot problem gets a lot more attention than a Sprint Review. No matter what size the organization, it is important to define the scope of sustaining tasks, identify who is responsible for handling any problems, and to make sure this information is properly presented in the Sprint Backlog.

There is a constant battle in most organizations between bringing the bug count down and developing new technology. Typically sustaining engineers report in through the development organization. Released products are managed through the Client Support organization. The Development Team is responsible for getting increments Done. Client Support is measured on the speed of turning around Clients questions. Client Support organizations want zero open bugs, this inherent conflict can cause problems. For a released product, Client Support, and the Development Manger need to clearly set guidelines for identifying what the bug classifications are, identifying what issues are truly a bug, and what is an enhancement.

If the Development Team is responsible for sustaining the product, it is important for them to keep track of the actual time they spend supporting sustaining efforts. This information will be funneled through the Sprint Backlog. It also needs to be given to the Project Manager since they can then factor it into the true cost of the product and provide justification for adding sustaining engineers.

Client Support needs to work with Development to identify which complaints are bugs, and which are actually feature enhancements. Feature enhancements need to be funneled to the Product Owner so they can be added to the Product Backlog.

Organizations also need to assure that training courses are available. Plus Client Support needs to be available and trained on the applications being supported.

Phase 5 – General Availability – Review Presentation

The Project Team should present the product's status to executive staff on a yearly basis.
- The Project Manager performs a 360 evaluation. That is all the suppositions made in Phase 1 are outlined in a column of a table next to their actual costs and revenue. This is used so the organization can better plan.
- Client Support or the Development Team presents the current bug count and reviews the actual man-hours spent sustaining the product.
- Client Support reviews the number of calls they receive.
- Product Marketing discusses actual market penetration and customer acceptance.
- Training presents their costs and effectiveness.
- Executive staff reviews this information and decides if this product should be funded for another year or if the product should be taken off the market and an end of life (EOL) review presented.

Sample Phase 5 Presentation Outline:

Page 1: This document should be controlled distribution, list the names of all the people attending and receiving the review handout. The cover page should have the product name, the phase, and the date.

Page 2: Agenda. List what will be presenting, the time allotted. Agenda items for a Phase 5 review may include an introduction, actual costs, bug listing, client's acceptance, and summary

Page 3: Review the items that have been created or completed over the past year including :
- Clients acceptance
- Outstanding bugs
- Future development
- Maintenance record
- Available training
- Marketing Communications

- Client Support availability – e.g. number of people trained on the product, number of clients questions on this product, speed of answering client's questions.

Page 4: Clients acceptance and status

Page 5: 360 Evaluation – comparing suppositions made in Phase 1 and Phase 2 with actual numbers

Page 6: Marketing Communications – advertising, blogging, social media, trade shows, industry conferences

Page 7: Financial Summary: list actual cost to sustain

Page 8: Executive Session: Executive sign-off, Executives note any action items and decide if this product should continue or be discontinued.

Recommendations for Management and Team Members

Management recommendations:
- Take phase reviews seriously – Phase reviews are designed to give executive management a "snapshot" of the status of the product. They are an excellent tool for confirming that processes are being followed and team deliverables are completed on time. If the Executives don't take phase reviews seriously, no one else will.
- Hold people accountable, track phase review promises – Phase reviews are an excellent way to monitor and track accountability. Save phase review presentations so you can track promises and commitments.
- Don't forget to review generally available products
- 360 review – comparing Phase 1 to actual costs and sales provides management an excellent tool for identifying how realistic the Phase 1 & 2 process is. This information can be used to assure that future projects have a better chance of meeting targets.
- Don't assume that the numbers are less favorable than originally predicted. Many times the acceptance of a product is more favorable than anyone ever predicted.

Team Member's Roles

- Development Manager
- Project manager

- Client Support
- Training Manger
- Marketing Communications

Development Team Phase 5 – General Availability
- Fixes bugs
- Maintains product if applicable
- Attends phase review

Project Manager Phase 5 – General Availability
- Compares Phase 1 and 2 suppositions to actuals
- Presents current status to Executive staff (Phase 5 review)

Client Support Phase 5 – General Availability
- Outlines open bugs and recommended features
- Outlines costs for supporting clients
- Attends phase review

Training Phase 5 – General availability
- Training is available
- Identifies training penetration and effectiveness
- Attends phase review

Marketing Communications Phase 5 – General availability
- Presents ongoing marketing activities and their effectiveness
- Attends phase review

Documents Created In Phase 5

- Executive Sign Off
- Phase Review Presentation

Executive Sign Off – This is a sign off the sheet the Project Manager presents to the Executives in the phase review. At the end of each phase review presentation, each member of the Executive staff reviews the phase sign off's, reflects on the information presented and decides if they agree to allow the product to proceed to the next stage of the product lifecycle. On the bottom of this document each executive signs his/her name and states if he/she approves or disapproves continuing to the next phase.

Phase Review Presentation – given to executive staff.

Phase 6 – End of Life

End of Life (EOL) is the process whereby the product history can be reviewed and a decision made regarding whether or not a product should be discontinued.
　At some point a product:
- Becomes obsolete
- Too expensive to support
- A better mousetrap has been invented.

The people involved with creating an end of life report are:
- Product Marketing
- Project Manager
- Client Support

　Product Marketing – gathers appropriate data for the presentation including, sales history and contractual obligations to support the product.
　Project Manager – Gathers cost for sustaining the product including Development, Dales, and Client Support. The Project Manager works with Product Marketing and Client Support to pull together data needed for the EOL presentation.
　Client Support – gathers support costs and Client interaction history over time.

What Happens During End of Life

　Organizations tend to overlook EOL. Many products silently slip into the night as newer products take their place. Organizations fail to take into account all of the hidden costs of maintaining a product such as sustaining development, training, and assuring there are knowledgeable Client Support people available. Products that are not being used can impact the efficiency of an organization.
　Many times management is not aware if a product is costing the organization more money to support than what it brings in. Or an old obsolete product can confuse customers. By creating an EOL presentation, information necessary for successful business decisions can be made. For products draining cash, management can make an informed decision to "pull the plug".
　There are many reasons to end a product including, the product costs more to support than new applications, clients have not been forced to migrate to a new application, the technology has become obsolete, and the product is expensive to support. Additionally, old products can confuse new customers.

Typically new products render an existing product obsolete. Many times the old product is automatically EOL when the new release becomes available. If this is not true, an the old product at some time needs to be EOL.

During EOL, the Project Manager reviews the product's financial history, comparing forecasted costs to actual costs. The Project Manager prepares a statement defining why the product is being EOL. Then recommends how to pull the plug.

Client Support's Role in EOL: Client Support has the key position in EOL. During EOL Client Support prepares a list of all the current Clients and cost of supporting these clients. Client Support's cost should including development's sustaining efforts. Client Support creates a plan that outlines how they will discontinue support. Example: Existing Clients need to be notified that as of a pre-determined date the product will no longer be supported.

Product Marketing works with Legal/Contract administrator to review all existing contracts to assure there are no legal reasons to continue supporting the product. If there are contracts that stipulate the continued support of a precut, the organization can decide to stop selling the product but still support the product.

Executive staff is responsible for approving a product for EOL.

Phase 6 – EOL Presentation

- Product Marketing creates an impact study. This study identifies the impact of discontinuing this product
- The Project Manager reviews any outstanding contracts and the cost/savings to cancel the product.
- Client Support reviews the cost of supporting the product and the cost/savings to discontinue the product

Sample Phase 6 presentation outline:

Page 1: Cover Page. This document should be controlled distribution, list the names of all the people attending and receiving the review handout. The cover page should have the product name, the phase, and the date.

Page 2: Agenda. List major deliverables for this phase, which team members will be presenting, the time allotted for presentations. Agenda items for a Phase 6 review may include: introduction, reason to EOL, Sustaining costs, Contracts

Page 3: Phase 6 – EOL: Review the items that have been created or completed in a Phase 6 EOL:

- Impact study
- Contract review status
- Clients notification

Page 4: Reason for EOL
Page 5: Install Base Status
Page 6: Financial Summary: Sustaining Costs, Contract Costs, Cost to EOL
Page 7: Recommendations

Recommendations for Management and Team Members

- Take phase reviews seriously – Phase reviews are designed to give Executives a "snapshot" onto the status of the product. If the Executive staff doesn't' take phase reviews seriously no one else will.

Team Member's Roles

- Project Manager
- Product Marketing
- Client Support

Product Marketing Phase 6 – EOL
- Performs impact study
- Attends phase review

Project Manager Phase 6 – EOL
- Receives impact study from Product Marketing
- Works with Legal to review contracts that refer to this product
- Presents EOL plan to Executive staff (Phase 6 review)
- Works with Client Support to notify clients of product's status

Client Support Phase 6 – EOL
- Creates study on existing support calls and breadth and depth of sustaining activity.
- Notifies Clients product has been EOL
- Attends phase review

Documents Created In Phase 6

- Executive Sign Off
- Phase Review presentation
- Phase sign off

Executive Sign Off – At the end of each phase review presentation, each member of the Executive staff reflects on the information presented and decides if they agree to allow the product to proceed to the next stage of the product lifecycle. On the bottom of this document each Executive signs his/her name and states if they approve or disapprove of continuing to the next phase.

Index

Scrum Definitions:

Burn Down – The trend of development work remaining across time in a Sprint, a Release, or a Product.

Daily Scrum – A short daily meeting facilitated by the Scrum Master where each member of the Development Team provides what they did the day before, what they will do that day, and what roadblocks they have.

Development Team – A cross-function team of three to nine members

Done – a mutually agreed upon definition of what it takes to complete an Item.

Epic – Are a group of Stories that comprise a complete workflow for a user.

Hardening Sprint - In a Hardening Sprint the Development Team doesn't create any new increments, instead they stabilize or integrate the product for release.

Increment – Functionality developed by the Team during each Sprint that is potentially shippable.

Item – Stories are broken down and turned into Items. Items include functional requirements, non-functional requirements, and issues, prioritized in order of importance.

Product Backlog – A prioritized list of requirements for the product.

Product Owner – The person responsible for representing the client, other stakeholders and managing the Product Backlog.

Scrum – Scrum is an iterative and incremental Agile software development framework for managing product development.

ScrumMaster – The person responsible for facilitating the Scrum process.

Sprint – A development cycle of one to four weeks.

Sprint Planning meeting – A meeting that kicks off each Sprint.

Sprint Backlog – A list of the Development Team's work for a Sprint.

Sprint Retrospective meeting – A meeting facilitated by the ScrumMaster where the Development Team determines how to make Sprints more productive.

Sprint Review meeting – At the end of every Sprint, the Development Team demonstrates the functionality they created.

Story – A story is a self-contained unit of work agreed upon by the developers and the stakeholders. A Story can be a single feature of a product.

Technical Debt – work that needs to be done before a particular job can be considered complete or proper.

Themes - Are different then an Epic. Like an Epic they are groups of related Stories. However, while some Stories in a Theme may be dependent on one another, they do not need to encapsulate a specific workflow or be delivered together.

Time box – A predetermined period of time that cannot be exceeded.

Phases in the Process

Phase 1 – Initiation – All ideas must be vetted. Initiation is the stage when the Business Plan is created and presented. The objective of Phase 1 is to introduce a new product idea or next generation idea to the organization, to gain agreement on relevance to strategic direction, to produce a Business Plan whereby executive staff receives a snapshot of the products costs, market reach, features, scope, and potential revenue. This way management can decide if it's beneficial for the organization to fund this product.

Phase 2 – Planning – The objective of Phase 2 is to define, architect, prototype, and design a product that satisfies the business plan identified in Phase 1. In Phase 2 the product architecture, a Development Cost Baseline and a Project Team is formed.

Phase 3 – Scrum-Development – Following the Scrum framework, the Development Team creates increments of the product by choosing items off of the prioritized Product Backlog. Each increment will work within the structure of the design created in Phase 2. The Development Team is responsible for creating, testing and quality assuring that each increment works to the definition of Done that has been mutually agreed on by all parties. After each increment has met the definition of Done, the Project Team will identify if the increment is ready to be released to Beta.

Phase 4 – Beta –After the Project Team decides that an increment, story, or epic is ready to be released, it is made available to a select group of clients who have agreed to confirm that the features work in a production environment.

Phase 5 – General Availability – After the Beta, when the team has confirmed that the increment works in a production environment the increment becomes generally available.

Phase 6 – End of Life – At the yearly product review meeting, management may decide that the product has become obsolete or more expensive to support than the benefit generated from use. End of Life is the process whereby the product's history can be reviewed and a decision can be made regarding whether or not a product should be discontinued.

Product Team Members

- Client Support Manager – is responsible for defining, designing, and developing a detailed plan that articulates how their organization will support a product after it's released. The Support Plan defines how Client Support staff will be trained, clients will access help, how bugs will be tracked and fixed after release, the training available to clients, and how updates/fixes will be sent to clients.
- Development Manager – representing the Architect who is responsible to design and architect the project and responsible for providing costing information.
- Documentation Manger – is the functional area responsible for all internal and client related documentation. The manager attends Project Team meetings, provides a Documentation Plan and costing information.
- Marketing Communications – is the functional area responsible for all communications inside and outside of the organization. They develop a Marketing Communications plan and provide costing information, and attend meetings.
- Product Marketing – is responsible for product direction, industry analysis, and competitive analysis, understanding the client's needs, and identifying and driving product direction. Product Marketing works with all areas within the organization to make sure the product is focused on the client's needs and is presented in the best possible light. Product Marketing is responsible for assuring the Business Plan is kept current.
- Project Manager – is responsible for managing the process, keeps the team focused on the product's goals and confirms that deliverables within each stage of the product lifecycle have been met. The Project Manager facilitates communications between team members and among departments. When deliverables slip it is the responsibility of the Project Manager to escalate this information and to facilitate resolution. In smaller organizations, the Product Manager's duties usually incorporate those of Product Marketing and Marketing Communications.
- Quality Assurance Manager - is the functional area responsible for assuring products meet corporate quality and the definition of Done. The manager attends Project Team meetings, provides a QA Plan and costing information.
- Training Manger – produces any classroom or online training needed for the product. The manager attends Project Team meetings, provides a Training Plan and costing information.

Documents Created by Phase

Phase 1: Initiation

Business Plan: Feasibility, Goal, Client's Needs, Product Environment, Product Backlog, Estimated Product Costs, Potential Revenue

Phase 2: Planning

Design Document – This is a detailed architectural document created to explain the scope of the product along with the detail design specifications that will be implementing in the development phase of the product lifecycle.

Team Minutes – The team minutes are updated after each meeting. They record details on commitments, status, issues, requests, road blocks, and team decisions. They should be updated and published within 24 hours of a Project Team meeting.

Client Support Plan – The Client Support department develops a document that details what and how they will support the product, track bugs, provide services to clients and update clients with fixes.

Communications Plan – Marketing Communications creates a plan that identifies the PR, Advertising, articles, and promotions anticipated for this product.

Development Plan – The Development Manager identifies the number of developers needed to develop the product, skill sets and training is included in this plan.

Document Plan – Documentation creates a plan that outlines what documents will be developed, the scope of each document. Documentation needs to create a detailed outline that defines each of the chapters within the document and items this will be addressed within each chapter.

Launch Plan – Product Marketing creates a plan that identifies the material they will develop for Sales (presentations), collateral (brochures, white papers) Web updates, customer stories, presentations at conferences, and customer tours.

QA Plan – The QA manager creates a plan that identifies how they will QA the product. What the quality standards are, and how they will assure quality standards are met.

Roll Out Plan – created by the Project Manager if hardware purchased from 3rd party sources is part of the Client solution. This includes targets for receiving, staging,

and installing the equipment along with targets of when vendors need to be chosen and estimated ship dates.
- Training Plan – Training will meet with Client Support and Product Marketing to assure knowledge of the intended Client. They will create a plan that identifies type and scope of training programs for the product.
- Development Cost Baseline –Each department provides the Project Manager with their expected costs. This information is used to updated the Baseline Cost Document created in Phase 1.
- Integrated Schedule –This is a detailed schedule that can be developed using a computer based scheduling application that details all the deliverables, interdependencies, start and complete dates of each department highlighting all of the processes necessary to create this product.
- Phase review presentation – presented to executive staff.
- Executive Sign Off – At the end of each phase review presentation, each member of the Executive staff reviews the phase sign off's, reflects on the information presented and decides if they agree to allow the product to proceed to the next stage of the product lifecycle. On the bottom of this document each executive signs his/her name and states if he/she approves or disapproves continuing to the next phase.
- Phase Sign Off: The team reviews their phase deliverables and agree if they've been completed and the project is ready to move to phase 3.

Phase 3: Scrum Development

Beta Plan – Created: The Beta plan is a document developed by Product Marketing and QA. The purpose of a Beta plan is to define the roles and responsibilities the people participating in the Beta process. The Beta plan details qualifications to become a Beta site along with technologies and procedures the Beta sites will be testing.

Beta Questionnaire – Created: The survey questions given to clients' needs to be created.

Escalation Procedures – The QA Manger works with Client Support to develops a detailed plan outlining escalation procedures and definitions for bug severity.

The Release Plan – Product Marketing produces a plan that identifies the procedure of moving Increments to Beta and Release

The Announcement Plan – Marketing Communications works with Product Marketing to identify which Stories or Epics will be announced and the level of announcement for each Story.

Sources Sited in this Book:

Wikipedia, The Scrum Guide, and The Scrum Primer were used as source documents and inspiration for Phase 3 – Scrum-Development.

Wikipedia: The free encyclopedia. (2004, July 22). FL: Wikimedia Foundation, Inc. Retrieved January 3, 2017, from https://www.wikipedia.org/wiki/Scrum_(software_development)

The Scrum Guide English (TM July 2016) – Ken Schwaber & Jeff Sutherland. http://www.scrumguides.org/

The Scrum Primer 2.0 English (© 2012) – Pete Deemer, Gabrielle Benefield, Craig Larman, Bas Vodde. http://scrumprimer.org/scrumprimer20.pdf

Printed in Great Britain
by Amazon